"The Business Acquisition Strategy"

Introduction

Biography: Arlind Sadiku

Chapter 1: Preparing for the Sale

Chapter 2: Valuing Your Business

Chapter 3: Financing

Chapter 4: The Team

Chapter 5: Meet The Buyers

Chapter 6: Marketing in M&A

Chapter 7: Meetings of the Minds

Chapter 8: The Offer

Chapter 9: The Due Diligence

Chapter 10: The Closing

Final Thoughts

M&A Acronyms and Language

Introduction

In today's dynamic business landscape, mergers and acquisitions (M&A) have emerged as pivotal strategies for business owners, investors, and entrepreneurs seeking growth, expansion, or exit opportunities. The intricacies involved in navigating the M&A process, from initial negotiations to closing the deal, are manifold and often daunting. It is in this context that my book,"The Business Acquisition Strategy" A Comprehensive Guide from Searching to Closing," becomes an indispensable resource for all stakeholders involved in M&A transactions.

At its core, M&A transactions are complex endeavors that require meticulous planning, strategic foresight, and adept execution. For business owners considering selling their company, understanding the nuances of the M&A process is crucial for maximizing value, mitigating risks, and ensuring a seamless transition. Conversely, investors and entrepreneurs seeking to acquire or invest in businesses must grasp the intricacies of due diligence, deal structuring, and post-closing integration to capitalize on opportunities effectively.

"The Business Acquisition Strategy" serves as a comprehensive roadmap that guides readers through every stage of the M&A journey, from the initial planning phase to the final closing. By offering practical insights, actionable strategies, and real-world examples, the book equips readers with the knowledge and tools needed to navigate the complexities of M&A transactions with confidence and clarity.

One of the key reasons why business owners, investors, and entrepreneurs need to read my book is its holistic approach to the M&A process. Unlike other resources that may focus on specific aspects of M&A, such as valuation or legal considerations, "The Business Acquisition Strategy"provides a comprehensive overview that covers all facets of the transaction. From conducting due diligence to negotiating the purchase agreement and beyond, each chapter delves into critical topics, offering practical advice and best practices gleaned from years of experience in the field.

""The Business Acquisition Strategy" is tailored to address the needs and concerns of a diverse audience, ranging from seasoned dealmakers to first-time sellers or buyers. Whether you are a business owner contemplating an exit strategy, an investor seeking to expand your portfolio, or an entrepreneur exploring growth opportunities through acquisition, the book offers valuable insights and actionable guidance that can be applied to your specific situation.

"The Business Acquisition Strategy" goes beyond mere theoretical concepts, providing readers with real-world case studies and anecdotes that illustrate key principles and lessons learned. By drawing on actual experiences and scenarios, the book offers readers a practical perspective on the challenges and opportunities inherent in M&A transactions, enabling them to anticipate potential pitfalls and navigate the process more effectively.

"The Business Acquisition Strategy" is not just a book; it is a comprehensive guide and strategic companion for anyone involved in the M&A arena. Whether you are embarking on your first deal or seeking to refine your existing M&A strategy, this book will empower you with the knowledge, insights, and tools needed to succeed in today's competitive business environment. From beginning to closing, "The Business Acquisition Strategy" is your roadmap to achieving M&A success.

Biography

Arlind "Alex" Sadiku is a multifaceted entrepreneur renowned for his visionary leadership and unwavering dedication to business innovation. With a fervent passion for technology and a keen eye for emerging trends, Alex embarked on his entrepreneurial journey with the establishment of Lunar Marketing, a dynamic firm offering bespoke marketing solutions to a diverse clientele.

Building upon his early success, Arlind co-founded Lunar Solutions, a pioneering software development company at the forefront of innovation in the hospitality sector. Through groundbreaking technologies and tailored solutions, Lunar Solutions transformed the industry landscape, earning acclaim for its forward-thinking approach and commitment to excellence. Driven by a relentless pursuit of growth and opportunity, Arlind co-founded the Aurora Consulting Group, where he provided strategic counsel to businesses navigating the complexities of expansion and success. Despite encountering challenges, such as the 2008 housing crisis, Arlind's resilience and strategic vision enabled him to pivot successfully, redirecting his focus to the flourishing hospitality sector. With the establishment of the Restaurant Investment Group, Alex facilitated the buying and selling of restaurants, spearheading successful culinary ventures in vibrant cities across the United States. His expertise in mergers and acquisitions propelled him to forge profitable partnerships between investors and entrepreneurs, further solidifying his reputation as a savvy businessman with a knack for identifying lucrative opportunities. Expanding his reach internationally, Arlind ventured into commercial real estate in Texas and later expanded his ventures to the cosmopolitan hub of London, UK. With a global perspective and a steadfast commitment to excellence, Arlind continues to serve as a trusted adviser to aspiring entrepreneurs and influential investors, empowering them to navigate the complexities of the business landscape with confidence and achieve lasting success. Arlind is Author of this book and other business related entrepreneurship books available on Amazon and Google.

Arlind Sadiku
Author / Entrepreneur / M&A
www.arlindsadiku.com

Chapter 1: Preparing for the Sale

Preparing a business for sale is akin to laying the groundwork for a successful journey into the market. It's a meticulous process that demands attention to detail, strategic planning, and a clear understanding of the business's strengths and weaknesses. This preparatory phase is not merely a formality; it's the cornerstone upon which the entire sale hinges.

At its core, preparing a business for sale is about striking a delicate balance between preparation and execution. While the execution phase may seem more glamorous, it's the preparation that sets the stage for success. Think of it as building a sturdy foundation for a house; without it, the entire structure risks collapse.

Thorough groundwork is essential in this process. It involves evaluating every aspect of the business, from its financial health to its operational efficiency, market positioning, and potential for growth. This comprehensive assessment helps identify areas of strength and weakness, enabling the business owner to address any shortcomings proactively.

Without adequate preparation, the execution phase of the sale may falter. Imagine trying to navigate a treacherous path without a map or compass; the chances of getting lost or encountering obstacles are significantly higher. Similarly, without a well-prepared business, the sale process can become mired in uncertainties, delays, and missed opportunities.

Moreover, insufficient preparation can jeopardize the chances of a sale altogether. Potential buyers are discerning; they scrutinize every aspect of the business before making a decision. If key information is missing, financial records are disorganized, or operational inefficiencies are apparent, buyers may lose confidence and walk away from the deal.

Therefore, thorough preparation is not just advisable; it's imperative. It's about mitigating risks, maximizing value, and positioning the business for success in the marketplace. It's about presenting the business in the best possible light, highlighting its strengths, and addressing any weaknesses head-on.

Preparing a business for sale is a meticulous process that requires careful planning, attention to detail, and a proactive approach. It's the foundation upon which the entire sale rests, and neglecting it can have dire consequences. By investing time and effort into preparation, business owners can increase their chances of a successful transaction and achieve their desired outcomes in the market.

Understanding why a business might not sell is a crucial step in the preparation process for any sale. It involves a comprehensive evaluation of the business's strengths and weaknesses, market position, and overall appeal to potential buyers. By identifying potential obstacles early on, business owners can take proactive measures to address them, thereby increasing the business's chances of a successful sale and maximizing its market value.

One of the primary reasons why a business might fail to attract buyers is poor financial performance. Buyers are inherently risk-averse and seek businesses with a track record of profitability and financial stability. If a business has a history of declining revenues, inconsistent cash flow, or unsustainable expenses, potential buyers may view it as too risky an investment. Therefore, it's essential for business owners to conduct a thorough financial analysis and identify areas for improvement. Implementing strategies to improve profitability, reduce costs, and enhance cash flow can significantly enhance the business's appeal to potential buyers and increase its market value.

Another common reason why a business might struggle to sell is a lack of differentiation. In today's competitive marketplace, businesses need to stand out from the crowd and offer something unique to attract buyers. If a business lacks a clear value proposition or fails to differentiate itself from competitors, potential buyers may view it as just another commodity, thereby diminishing its appeal. Therefore, it's crucial for business owners to identify and articulate their unique selling points and leverage them to position the business as a desirable investment opportunity. Whether it's innovative products or services, a strong brand identity, or a loyal customer base, highlighting these strengths can significantly enhance the business's appeal to potential buyers and increase its market value.

Inadequate documentation is another common obstacle that can hinder the sale of a business. Potential buyers rely on comprehensive and accurate documentation to evaluate the business's financial health, operational efficiency, and growth potential. If key documents such as financial statements, contracts, leases, and intellectual property rights are incomplete, outdated, or poorly organized, potential buyers may question the business's credibility and legitimacy. Therefore, it's essential for business owners to ensure that all relevant documentation is up-to-date, accurate, and readily accessible. Investing time and resources in organizing and preparing these documents can significantly enhance the business's appeal to potential buyers and increase its market value.

Understanding why a business might not sell is a critical aspect of the preparation process for any sale. By identifying potential weaknesses such as poor financial performance, lack of differentiation, or inadequate documentation, business owners can take proactive measures to address them and increase the business's appeal to potential buyers. By addressing these issues early on, business owners can maximize the business's market value and increase its chances of a successful sale.

Increasing a business's value is a pivotal aspect of preparing it for sale, and it requires a multifaceted approach aimed at enhancing its appeal to potential buyers. This process involves implementing strategic initiatives to optimize operations, strengthen customer relationships, and diversify revenue streams. By enhancing its overall value proposition, a business can not only attract more interest from prospective buyers but also command a higher selling price in the market.

Optimizing operations is one of the primary strategies for increasing a business's value. Efficient and streamlined operations not only improve profitability but also make the business more attractive to potential buyers. This may involve streamlining workflows, reducing inefficiencies, and implementing technology solutions to automate processes. By optimizing operations, businesses can demonstrate their ability to generate consistent revenue and maintain sustainable growth, thereby enhancing their appeal to prospective buyers.

Strengthening customer relationships is another crucial strategy for increasing a business's value. A loyal and satisfied customer base is a valuable asset that can significantly enhance the perceived value of a business. Building strong relationships with customers through exceptional service, personalized experiences, and effective communication can not only drive revenue but also increase customer retention and loyalty. Businesses with a loyal customer base are more likely to attract interest from prospective buyers who see the potential for continued growth and profitability.

Diversifying revenue streams is also essential for increasing a business's value. Relying too heavily on a single product or service can make a business vulnerable to market fluctuations and changes in consumer preferences. By diversifying revenue streams, businesses can spread risk and create new opportunities for growth. This may involve expanding into new markets, launching complementary products or services, or developing alternative revenue models. Businesses with diversified revenue streams are more resilient and attractive to potential buyers who seek stability and growth potential.

Ultimately, enhancing a business's value proposition is about showcasing its strengths and potential for future success. By implementing strategic initiatives to optimize operations, strengthen customer relationships, and diversify revenue streams, businesses can position themselves as attractive investment opportunities in the eyes of prospective buyers. A strong value proposition not only attracts more interest but also enables businesses to command a higher selling price, maximizing the return on investment for business owners.

Increasing a business's value is a critical component of preparing it for sale. By focusing on strategies to optimize operations, strengthen customer relationships, and diversify revenue streams, businesses can enhance their appeal to potential buyers and command a higher selling price in the market. By investing in initiatives that increase value, business owners can maximize their returns and achieve successful outcomes in the sale process.

Informing and retaining employees during the sale process is paramount to maintaining stability and preserving morale within an organization. The transition of ownership or management can be a time of uncertainty and anxiety for employees, and effective communication and transparency are essential to alleviate concerns and foster a sense of trust.

Open communication is key to keeping employees informed throughout the sale process. From the initial announcement of the sale to updates on the progress and eventual outcome, employees should be kept in the loop regarding any developments that may affect them. This not only demonstrates respect for their role within the organization but also helps to dispel rumors and speculation that can breed uncertainty and erode morale.

Transparency is equally important in ensuring that employees feel valued and respected during the sale process. Providing honest and accurate information about the reasons for the sale, the potential impact on employees, and the plans for the future can help to alleviate fears and build confidence in the new ownership or management. Transparency also allows employees to ask questions and voice concerns, fostering a sense of empowerment and involvement in the transition process.

Maintaining stability within the organization is essential for minimizing disruptions and ensuring continued productivity during the sale process. When employees feel uncertain about their future with the company, they may become disengaged or seek opportunities elsewhere, leading to talent attrition and loss of institutional knowledge. By keeping employees informed and engaged, businesses can reduce the risk of turnover and preserve the continuity of operations throughout the transition period. Preserving morale is another critical aspect of retaining employees during the sale process. Uncertainty and anxiety can take a toll on employee morale, leading to decreased motivation, increased stress, and diminished performance. Open communication, transparency, and reassurance can help to mitigate these effects by demonstrating empathy and understanding for employees' concerns and providing them with the support they need to navigate the transition successfully. Informing and retaining employees during the sale process is essential for maintaining stability and preserving morale within an organization. Open communication and transparency are key to alleviating concerns and fostering a sense of trust among employees, reducing the risk of talent attrition, and ensuring a smooth transition for all parties involved. By keeping employees informed, engaged, and reassured throughout the sale process, businesses can minimize disruptions and preserve the continuity of operations, ultimately contributing to the long-term success of the organization.

Organizing key documents and normalizing financial statements are fundamental steps in preparing a business for sale. These tasks are critical because buyers heavily rely on these documents to assess the financial health, operational efficiency, and growth potential of the business. By ensuring that all relevant information is readily accessible and accurately presented, business owners can instill confidence in potential buyers and facilitate the due diligence process, ultimately increasing the likelihood of a successful sale.

Key documents such as financial statements, contracts, leases, intellectual property rights, and employee agreements provide valuable insights into the inner workings of a business. They offer potential buyers a comprehensive view of the company's financial performance, assets, liabilities, and legal obligations. Organizing these documents in a clear and systematic manner not only saves time but also demonstrates professionalism and attention to detail, which can leave a positive impression on prospective buyers.

Normalizing financial statements is equally important in preparing a business for sale. Normalization involves adjusting the financial statements to reflect the true economic performance of the business by removing any one-time or non-recurring expenses or revenues. This process allows potential buyers to make more accurate comparisons between different businesses and assess the true earning potential of the company. By presenting normalized financial statements, business owners can provide a clearer picture of the business's financial health and profitability, which can enhance its attractiveness to potential buyers. Ensuring that all relevant information is readily accessible and accurately

presented is crucial for instilling confidence in potential buyers. Buyers conduct thorough due diligence to assess the risks and opportunities associated with the business before making a purchase decision. By organizing key documents and presenting normalized financial statements, business owners make it easier for buyers to conduct due diligence and gain a comprehensive understanding of the business's operations, financial performance, and growth prospects. Furthermore, organized and normalized financial documents can help expedite the sale process and minimize delays. Potential buyers are more likely to move forward with a transaction if they have confidence in the accuracy and reliability of the information provided. By proactively organizing key documents and normalizing financial statements, business owners can demonstrate their commitment to transparency and facilitate smoother negotiations, ultimately increasing the likelihood of a successful sale.
Organizing key documents and normalizing financial statements are fundamental steps in preparing a business for sale. These tasks not only provide potential buyers with valuable insights into the business's financial health, operational efficiency, and growth potential but also instill confidence and facilitate due diligence processes. By ensuring that all relevant information is readily accessible and accurately presented, business owners can increase the attractiveness of their business to potential buyers and maximize their chances of achieving a successful sale.
Despite thorough preparation, some businesses may still encounter challenges when attempting to sell. These hurdles can arise from a variety of factors, including unfavorable market conditions, industry-specific challenges, or unrealistic valuation expectations. Understanding and addressing these obstacles are crucial for business owners to navigate the complexities of the sales process effectively and increase their chances of achieving a successful transaction.
Unfavorable market conditions can significantly impact the sale of a business. Economic downturns, industry disruptions, or changes in consumer behavior can create uncertainty and reduce buyer interest. In such cases, business owners may need to adjust their timing and approach to selling, considering factors such as market trends, competition, and potential buyers' financial capabilities. Additionally, positioning the business as a resilient and adaptable investment

opportunity despite market challenges can help attract interested buyers and mitigate concerns about risk.

Industry-specific challenges can also pose obstacles to selling a business. Factors such as regulatory changes, technological advancements, or shifts in consumer preferences can affect the perceived value of a business within its industry. Business owners need to stay informed about industry trends and developments and position their business to capitalize on emerging opportunities or mitigate potential risks. This may involve diversifying revenue streams, investing in innovation, or adapting business models to align with changing market dynamics.

Unrealistic valuation expectations are another common barrier to selling a business. Business owners may overestimate the value of their business based on personal attachment, emotional investment, or optimistic projections. However, inflated valuations can deter potential buyers and prolong the sales process. It's essential for business owners to conduct thorough market research, seek professional valuation advice, and set realistic expectations about the value of their business. By aligning their valuation expectations with market realities, business owners can attract more qualified buyers and increase their chances of completing a successful sale.

Understanding these obstacles is critical for business owners preparing to sell their businesses. By recognizing the potential challenges posed by unfavorable market conditions, industry-specific factors, or unrealistic valuation expectations, business owners can adjust their strategies accordingly and position their businesses for success in the sales process. Whether it involves timing the sale to coincide with more favorable market conditions, addressing industry-specific challenges through strategic initiatives, or setting realistic valuation expectations, proactive planning and adaptation are essential for navigating the complexities of selling a business effectively. With a clear understanding of these obstacles and a strategic approach to addressing them, business owners can increase their chances of achieving a successful sale and realizing their desired outcomes.

Chapter 2: Valuing Your Business

Valuing a business accurately is a pivotal step in the sale process, serving as the bedrock upon which negotiations and strategic decisions are built. For both buyers and sellers, the valuation is more than just a number; it's a critical factor that influences the terms of the deal, the perceived value of the business, and the ultimate success of the transaction. However, achieving a precise valuation is often easier said than done, given the multitude of factors and methodologies involved in the process.

At its core, business valuation is a complex interplay of quantitative analysis, qualitative assessments, and market dynamics. Numerous factors come into play, including the company's financial performance, growth prospects, industry trends, competitive landscape, and economic conditions. Additionally, the choice of valuation methodology—from income-based approaches like discounted cash flow (DCF) analysis to market-based methods like comparable company analysis—can significantly impact the final valuation figure.

Understanding these intricacies is paramount for stakeholders involved in the sale process. For sellers, an accurate valuation ensures they receive fair market value for their business, maximizing returns on their investment and providing a solid foundation for their post-sale endeavors. On the other hand, buyers rely on valuations to assess the potential return on investment, evaluate the risks associated with the acquisition, and determine the appropriate purchase price.

A precise valuation facilitates transparent and constructive negotiations between buyers and sellers. Armed with a thorough understanding of the business's value drivers and potential areas of concern, both parties can engage in meaningful discussions aimed at reaching mutually beneficial agreements. Whether negotiating price adjustments, earn-outs, or contingent payments, a well-supported valuation empowers stakeholders to make informed decisions that align with their objectives and risk tolerance.

Beyond the negotiation table, an accurate valuation also plays a pivotal role in securing financing for the transaction. Lenders and investors often rely on the assessed value of the business as a key factor in their decision-making process. A credible valuation report can instill confidence in potential financiers, facilitating access to capital and expediting the closing process.

The importance of valuing a business accurately cannot be overstated in the context of a sale transaction. While the process may be fraught with challenges and complexities, a thorough understanding of the factors and methodologies involved is essential for achieving favorable outcomes. By investing the time and resources necessary to conduct a comprehensive valuation, stakeholders can mitigate risks, seize opportunities, and navigate the sale process with confidence and clarity.

The valuation of a business is not a straightforward process but rather a nuanced evaluation influenced by a myriad of factors. Among these factors, the subjective nature of certain elements plays a significant role in contributing to variations in valuation assessments. Market conditions, industry trends, and economic outlooks are all examples of subjective factors that can sway perceptions of value, thereby introducing discrepancies in valuation outcomes.

Market conditions exert a profound influence on how a business is valued. Fluctuations in supply and demand dynamics, investor sentiment, and overall economic stability can significantly impact perceptions of a company's worth. During periods of economic expansion, for instance, businesses may be valued more optimistically due to heightened investor confidence and a favorable business climate. Conversely, in times of economic downturn or uncertainty, valuations may trend downward as risk aversion increases and growth prospects dim.

Industry trends play a crucial role in shaping valuation assessments. Industries experiencing rapid growth or disruption may be valued more highly than those facing stagnation or decline. Technological advancements, regulatory changes, and shifts in consumer preferences can all influence the perceived value of a business within its respective industry. Moreover, the competitive landscape and barriers to entry within an industry can affect valuation multiples, with businesses operating in highly competitive markets often commanding lower valuations.

Economic outlooks, both at the macroeconomic and microeconomic levels, can influence perceptions of value. Factors such as interest rates, inflation rates, and geopolitical events can all impact investor confidence and risk perceptions, thereby affecting valuation assessments. Additionally, regional or sector-specific economic conditions can further contribute to variations in valuations, as businesses operating in different markets may be subject to unique economic pressures and opportunities.

In addition to subjective external factors, differences in methodologies and assumptions can also lead to variations in valuation conclusions. Various valuation approaches, such as the income approach, market approach, and asset-based approach, rely on different assumptions and inputs to derive a business's worth. Discrepancies in assumptions related to growth rates, discount rates, terminal values, and risk factors can result in divergent valuation outcomes, even when using the same methodology.

The subjective nature of certain factors, including market conditions, industry trends, and economic outlooks, as well as differences in methodologies and assumptions, contribute to variations in valuation assessments. Recognizing and understanding these factors is essential for stakeholders involved in the valuation process, as it allows for a more nuanced and informed approach to determining a business's worth. By considering the broader context and incorporating multiple perspectives, stakeholders can arrive at more comprehensive and defensible valuation conclusions, ultimately facilitating more informed decision-making in the realm of business transactions.

Cash flow serves as a cornerstone in evaluating the financial health and worth of a business. It represents the lifeblood of an enterprise, reflecting its ability to generate income, cover expenses, and sustain operations over time. As such, understanding and accurately assessing cash flow is paramount in determining a business's value. However, there is no one-size-fits-all approach to measuring cash flow, as different metrics offer distinct perspectives on a company's financial performance. Among the plethora of measures available, three stand out as the most common and widely used: EBITDA (Earnings Before Interest, Taxes, Depreciation, and Amortization), seller's discretionary earnings (SDE), and free cash flow (FCF).

EBITDA, often considered a proxy for operating cash flow, strips away non-operational expenses such as interest, taxes, depreciation, and amortization from a company's earnings. This metric provides insight into a business's core profitability, excluding the effects of financing decisions, accounting practices, and non-cash items. EBITDA is particularly favored in industries with heavy capital expenditures or significant depreciation charges, as it allows for a clearer comparison of operating performance across companies.

Seller's discretionary earnings (SDE), on the other hand, offers a more owner-centric view of cash flow. It reflects the total benefits enjoyed by a business owner, including pre-tax profits, owner's salary, perks, and non-recurring expenses. SDE is commonly used in small and owner-operated businesses, where owner involvement and discretionary expenses play a significant role in determining the company's value. This measure provides prospective buyers with a comprehensive understanding of the financial benefits associated with owning and operating the business.

Free cash flow (FCF) represents the cash generated by a business after accounting for capital expenditures necessary to maintain or expand its operations. FCF is a critical measure of a company's financial flexibility and ability to generate surplus cash for reinvestment, debt repayment, or distribution to shareholders. It reflects the cash available to stakeholders, irrespective of financing and accounting considerations, making it a valuable indicator of a business's intrinsic value and investment potential.

The choice of cash flow measure depends on the specific circumstances of the valuation and the nature of the business being evaluated. For large corporations with significant capital investments and complex capital structures, EBITDA may be the preferred measure for assessing operating performance. In contrast, SDE may be more suitable for small businesses or those heavily influenced by owner involvement and discretionary expenses. Meanwhile, FCF offers insights into a company's cash-generating ability and financial sustainability, making it a valuable metric in various valuation contexts.

Cash flow plays a pivotal role in determining a business's value, and the choice of cash flow measure can significantly impact valuation outcomes. EBITDA, SDE, and FCF each offer unique insights into a company's financial performance and profitability, catering to different valuation scenarios and business characteristics. By understanding the nuances of each measure and selecting the most appropriate one for the valuation at hand, stakeholders can make more informed decisions and arrive at more accurate assessments of a business's worth.

Selecting the right measure of cash flow is a critical component of conducting an accurate valuation of a business. While cash flow serves as a fundamental indicator of a company's financial performance and value, the choice of cash flow measure can significantly impact the valuation outcome. Factors such as the business's industry, growth trajectory, and capital structure play a crucial role in determining which measure is most appropriate for the valuation process. By aligning the valuation with the business's unique characteristics, stakeholders can obtain a more reliable estimate of its value.

One of the primary considerations when selecting a measure of cash flow is the industry in which the business operates. Different industries have distinct operating dynamics, capital requirements, and financial metrics that influence the choice of cash flow measure. For example, industries with high capital intensity or significant depreciation expenses may favor metrics like EBITDA, which focus on operating profitability and exclude non-operating expenses such as depreciation and amortization. On the other hand, service-based industries or businesses with minimal capital expenditures may prioritize measures like free cash flow (FCF), which provide a more accurate representation of cash available for reinvestment or distribution to stakeholders.

Additionally, the growth trajectory of the business plays a crucial role in determining the appropriate measure of cash flow for valuation purposes. Rapidly growing companies often reinvest a substantial portion of their earnings into expansion initiatives, resulting in lower reported earnings but higher free cash flow. In such cases, FCF may offer a more comprehensive picture of the company's financial performance and potential for future growth, as it accounts for capital expenditures necessary to sustain or accelerate growth. Conversely, mature businesses with stable cash flows and predictable earnings may rely on metrics like EBITDA or net income to assess their value, as they provide a clearer view of operating profitability and performance.

Furthermore, the capital structure of the business influences the choice of cash flow measure and the valuation methodology employed. Companies with high levels of debt or complex capital structures may prefer metrics like EBITDA, which focus on operating profitability and exclude financing-related expenses such as interest payments. By isolating operating performance from financing decisions, EBITDA provides a more accurate reflection of a company's core business value, particularly in leveraged buyout scenarios or debt-heavy industries.

Ultimately, aligning the valuation with the business's unique characteristics is essential for obtaining a more reliable estimate of its value. By considering factors such as industry dynamics, growth trajectory, and capital structure, stakeholders can select the most appropriate measure of cash flow for the valuation process. Whether assessing operating profitability, cash-generating ability, or financial sustainability, the right measure of cash flow ensures a more accurate and insightful valuation outcome, empowering stakeholders to make informed decisions and maximize value creation opportunities.

Valuing a business is a multifaceted process that requires careful consideration of various factors and methodologies. Among the plethora of valuation approaches available, three primary methods stand out as the most commonly used: the income approach, the market approach, and the asset-based approach. Each method relies on different principles and assumptions to derive a valuation, offering distinct perspectives on the business's worth. Understanding these methods and their underlying principles is essential for conducting comprehensive valuations that accurately reflect the intrinsic value of the business.

The income approach, also known as the earnings-based approach, focuses on the future income-generating potential of the business. This method involves estimating the present value of the business's expected future cash flows, discounted at an appropriate rate to reflect the time value of money and risk factors. The income approach is based on the principle that the value of a business is determined by its ability to generate profits over time, making it particularly suitable for businesses with predictable revenue streams and stable growth prospects. By forecasting future cash flows and discounting them back to present value, this method provides insight into the business's intrinsic value and investment potential.

In contrast, the market approach relies on comparisons with similar businesses that have been recently sold or are publicly traded. This method involves analyzing market transactions and pricing multiples within the relevant industry to estimate the value of the subject business. The market approach is based on the principle of market efficiency, assuming that the price paid for comparable businesses reflects their true market value. By benchmarking the subject business against comparable peers, this method provides a real-world indication of its value relative to the broader market. However, the market approach may be less reliable in industries with limited comparable data or unique business models.

The asset-based approach, also known as the cost approach, focuses on the value of the business's underlying assets. This method involves estimating the fair market value of the business's tangible and intangible assets, including property, equipment, inventory, intellectual property, and goodwill. The asset-based approach is based on the principle of asset substitution, assuming that investors would not pay more for the business than the cost of acquiring and replacing its assets. While this method provides a conservative estimate of the business's value, it may undervalue businesses with significant intangible assets or future earning potential.

Understanding these valuation methods and their underlying principles is essential for conducting comprehensive valuations that accurately reflect the intrinsic value of the business. By leveraging the strengths of each approach and considering the specific characteristics of the business and its industry, stakeholders can arrive at a more informed and defensible valuation conclusion. Whether assessing future income potential, market comparables, or asset values, a thorough understanding of valuation methodologies enables stakeholders to make strategic decisions and maximize value creation opportunities in the realm of business transactions.

Navigating the complexities of business valuation requires a deep understanding of key concepts and principles that underpin the valuation process. These concepts serve as the foundation upon which valuation methodologies are built, providing valuable insights into a business's financial performance, growth prospects, and intrinsic value. Mastery of these concepts is essential for stakeholders involved in the valuation process, as it can enhance the accuracy and reliability of valuation assessments, ultimately facilitating more informed decision-making and maximizing value creation opportunities. Here are ten valuation concepts that are crucial to understand:

Discounted Cash Flow (DCF) Analysis: DCF analysis is a method used to estimate the present value of a business's future cash flows. It involves forecasting future cash flows, discounting them back to present value using an appropriate discount rate, and calculating the net present value (NPV) of the business. DCF analysis is based on the principle that the value of a business is equal to the sum of its expected future cash flows, adjusted for the time value of money and risk factors.

Multiples Analysis: Multiples analysis involves comparing the valuation of a business to similar companies in the same industry using key financial metrics such as price-to-earnings (P/E) ratio, price-to-sales (P/S) ratio, or enterprise value-to-EBITDA (EV/EBITDA) ratio. This method relies on the principle of relative valuation, assuming that comparable companies trade at similar multiples of earnings, revenue, or other financial metrics.

Terminal Value: Terminal value represents the value of a business's cash flows beyond the explicit forecast period in a DCF analysis. It is typically estimated using a perpetual growth rate or a multiple of terminal cash flows. Terminal value accounts for the ongoing value of the business after the forecast period and is a critical component of DCF analysis.

Risk Assessment: Risk assessment involves evaluating the various risks that could impact a business's future cash flows and valuation. These risks may include industry risks, market risks, operational risks, financial risks, and macroeconomic risks. Understanding and quantifying these risks are essential for accurately assessing a business's value and determining an appropriate discount rate in DCF analysis.

Growth Projections: Growth projections involve forecasting a business's future revenue, earnings, and cash flows based on historical performance, market trends, and growth drivers. Growth projections are critical for estimating a business's future cash flows and assessing its potential for value creation over time.

Cost of Capital: The cost of capital represents the rate of return required by investors to compensate them for the risk of investing in a business. It is used as the discount rate in DCF analysis and reflects the weighted average cost of equity and debt financing. The cost of capital is influenced by factors such as the business's risk profile, capital structure, and prevailing market conditions.

Market Comparables: Market comparables involve benchmarking a business's valuation against similar companies in the same industry. This method relies on the principle of market efficiency, assuming that comparable companies trade at similar valuation multiples based on their financial performance, growth prospects, and risk profiles.

Synergies: Synergies refer to the additional value that can be created through the combination of two businesses in a merger or acquisition. These synergies may include cost savings, revenue enhancements, and other strategic benefits. Understanding and quantifying synergies are essential for accurately assessing the value of a potential transaction.

Liquidity Discounts: Liquidity discounts are adjustments made to a business's valuation to account for the lack of marketability or liquidity of its shares. Illiquid assets are typically valued at a discount compared to their liquid counterparts to compensate investors for the inability to quickly convert their investment into cash.

Control Premiums: Control premiums represent the additional value that a controlling shareholder is willing to pay for a business to gain control over its operations and decision-making. Control premiums are typically applied in the context of minority interest valuations or acquisition transactions where control of the business is being transferred.

Mastering these ten valuation concepts is essential for navigating the complexities of business valuation effectively. Whether conducting a DCF analysis, multiple analysis, or assessing market comparables, a thorough understanding of these concepts can enhance the accuracy and reliability of valuation assessments, enabling stakeholders to make informed decisions and maximize value creation opportunities.

Choosing the right appraiser is a critical decision that can have a profound impact on the outcome of the valuation process. An experienced and reputable appraiser, like Arlind Sadiku, brings invaluable expertise and insights to the table, significantly influencing the accuracy, credibility, and reliability of the valuation assessment. Whether assessing the value of a business, real estate property, or other assets, the appraiser plays a pivotal role in determining the fair market value and facilitating informed decision-making among stakeholders.

One of the primary reasons why selecting the right appraiser is crucial is the specialized knowledge and expertise they bring to the valuation process. An experienced appraiser, such as Arlind Sadiku, possesses industry-specific insights and understanding of valuation methodologies that enable them to navigate complex valuation challenges effectively. Whether evaluating a niche market, unique business model, or specialized asset class, Arlind's expertise ensures a thorough and accurate assessment that considers all relevant factors and nuances specific to the industry.

A reputable appraiser like Arlind brings credibility and trustworthiness to the valuation process, instilling confidence among stakeholders and enhancing the legitimacy of the valuation outcome. Arlind's track record of delivering high-quality valuations and adhering to professional standards and best practices reinforces the credibility of the valuation assessment, mitigating concerns and uncertainties surrounding the valuation process.

Evaluating qualifications, track record, and approach to valuation is essential for ensuring a rigorous and credible valuation outcome. By conducting due diligence on credentials, including certifications, licenses, and professional affiliations, stakeholders can verify his competency and adherence to ethical standards in the appraisal profession. Additionally, reviewing track record of past valuations and client testimonials provides insights into his expertise, reliability, and ability to deliver accurate and insightful valuation assessments.

Arlind's approach to valuation, including his methodology, assumptions, and valuation techniques, is another crucial aspect to consider when selecting an appraiser. By engaging Adam in a transparent and collaborative dialogue about the valuation process, stakeholders can gain a better understanding of his analytical framework, assumptions, and rationale behind the valuation assessment. This ensures alignment with stakeholders' objectives and expectations, fostering trust and confidence in the valuation outcome.

Choosing the right appraiser, such as Arlind, is a critical decision that can significantly impact the outcome of the valuation process. An experienced and reputable appraiser with industry-specific expertise and a thorough understanding of valuation methodologies brings invaluable insights and credibility to the valuation assessment. By evaluating Adam's qualifications, track record, and approach to valuation, stakeholders can ensure a rigorous and credible valuation outcome that facilitates informed decision-making and maximizes value creation opportunities.

Valuing a business is a complex and multifaceted undertaking that requires careful consideration of various factors and methodologies. By understanding the reasons for valuation variations, selecting the appropriate measures of cash flow, mastering valuation methods and concepts, and choosing the right appraiser, stakeholders can navigate the valuation process with confidence and precision, ultimately maximizing the value of their business transactions.

Chapter 3: Financing

Financing is the lifeblood of business transactions, serving as the fuel that propels growth, facilitates acquisitions, and enables ownership transfers. In the dynamic landscape of entrepreneurship, access to capital is paramount, empowering businesses to seize opportunities, navigate challenges, and realize their strategic objectives. Understanding the diverse sources of financing available is essential for entrepreneurs, as it equips them with the knowledge and resources needed to navigate the complexities of the financial landscape and execute their vision effectively.

At its core, financing plays a pivotal role in facilitating business transactions by providing the necessary capital to fund various activities. Whether it's expanding operations, investing in new technologies, or pursuing strategic partnerships, businesses rely on financing to fuel their growth trajectory. Without adequate capital, businesses may struggle to seize opportunities and remain competitive in today's fast-paced business environment.

One of the key functions of financing is to support acquisitions, allowing businesses to expand their footprint, diversify their offerings, and enter new markets. Acquisitions can be transformative for businesses, enabling them to consolidate market share, access new customer segments, and capitalize on synergies. However, successful acquisitions often require significant capital investment, making financing a critical component of the transaction process.

Financing plays a crucial role in ownership transfers, facilitating the transition of businesses from one owner to another. Whether it's selling a business outright, passing it down to family members, or transitioning ownership to employees, financing mechanisms such as seller financing and external loans can help facilitate smooth ownership transfers. These financing arrangements provide buyers with the capital needed to acquire businesses while offering sellers flexible payment terms and potential tax benefits.

Understanding the various sources of financing available empowers entrepreneurs to explore opportunities and execute strategic initiatives effectively. From traditional bank loans and lines of credit to alternative financing options such as venture capital, private equity, and crowdfunding, entrepreneurs have access to a diverse array of funding sources tailored to their specific needs and objectives. By assessing their financing options strategically, entrepreneurs can identify the most suitable sources of capital for their business ventures and optimize their financial resources for maximum impact.

Understanding the nuances of different financing sources enables entrepreneurs to mitigate risks and optimize financial structures to support their long-term growth objectives. By diversifying their sources of capital and leveraging a mix of debt and equity financing, businesses can achieve optimal capital structures that balance risk and return while maximizing flexibility and scalability.

Financing plays a pivotal role in facilitating business transactions, providing the necessary capital to fuel growth, acquisitions, and ownership transfers. By understanding the various sources of financing available and leveraging them strategically, entrepreneurs can empower themselves to explore opportunities, navigate challenges, and execute their vision effectively. In the dynamic landscape of entrepreneurship, access to capital is not just a financial necessity but a strategic imperative that drives innovation, expansion, and long-term success.

Selling a business is a significant decision that requires careful consideration of various factors, including the method of transaction. One option available to sellers is to pursue all-cash transactions, a straightforward approach that offers simplicity, certainty, and numerous benefits.

In an all-cash transaction, the buyer pays the entire purchase price upfront in cash, providing the seller with immediate liquidity and financial security. This immediate liquidity can be particularly advantageous for sellers who seek to liquidate their investment quickly or need funds to pursue other opportunities, such as starting a new venture or funding retirement plans. By receiving the full purchase price upfront, sellers can mitigate the risks associated with payment delays, financing contingencies, or potential defaults, thereby ensuring a smoother and more predictable transaction process.

Furthermore, all-cash deals streamline the transaction process by eliminating the complexities and uncertainties often associated with alternative financing arrangements. Without the need to secure external financing or negotiate terms with lenders, the transaction can proceed more expeditiously, reducing administrative burdens and accelerating the timeline to closing. This efficiency benefits both parties involved, enabling them to focus on the essential aspects of the transaction and minimize disruptions to ongoing business operations.

All-cash transactions provide sellers with the flexibility to pursue new ventures or retirement plans without the constraints of ongoing financial obligations or ownership responsibilities. Whether it's exploring new business opportunities, embarking on a personal passion project, or enjoying a well-deserved retirement, sellers can transition to the next phase of their lives with confidence and financial security. The immediate liquidity provided by an all-cash deal empowers sellers to make informed decisions about their future and seize new opportunities as they arise.

In addition to these benefits, all-cash transactions offer peace of mind to sellers by reducing the likelihood of transactional risks and uncertainties. With the entire purchase price paid upfront, sellers can avoid potential disputes or complications that may arise from deferred payments, financing issues, or buyer defaults. This certainty enhances the overall transaction experience for sellers, allowing them to navigate the process with confidence and peace of mind.

All-cash transactions offer numerous advantages to sellers seeking to sell their businesses efficiently and effectively. By providing simplicity, certainty, immediate liquidity, and flexibility, all-cash deals enable sellers to mitigate risks, streamline the transaction process, and pursue their financial goals with confidence. Whether it's funding new ventures, planning for retirement, or simply seeking peace of mind, all-cash transactions empower sellers to achieve their objectives and transition to the next chapter of their lives with confidence and financial security.

Seller financing, often referred to as owner financing, is a strategic approach to facilitating business sales that offers numerous benefits for both buyers and sellers. In this arrangement, the seller extends credit to the buyer to cover a portion of the purchase price, creating a unique financing mechanism that can enhance the transaction process and create value for all parties involved.

One of the primary advantages of seller financing is that it provides buyers with access to financing without relying solely on external lenders. Traditional financing arrangements, such as bank loans or lines of credit, may be inaccessible or cost-prohibitive for some buyers, particularly in cases where the business's financial performance or creditworthiness is not well-established. By offering seller financing, sellers can expand the pool of potential buyers and increase the likelihood of completing the sale, thereby maximizing their chances of achieving a favorable outcome.

Seller financing can benefit buyers by offering more flexible terms and conditions compared to traditional lending sources. Sellers have the flexibility to negotiate the terms of the financing arrangement, including interest rates, repayment schedules, and collateral requirements, based on their individual preferences and risk tolerance. This flexibility can be particularly advantageous for buyers who may face challenges obtaining financing through conventional channels or who prefer alternative financing options tailored to their specific needs and circumstances.

In addition to benefiting buyers, seller financing can also provide sellers with additional income streams and potential tax advantages. By extending credit to the buyer, sellers can generate ongoing cash flow in the form of interest payments, helping them achieve their financial goals and objectives over time. Moreover, seller financing can offer potential tax advantages for sellers, such as the ability to spread capital gains tax liability over multiple years or take advantage of favorable tax treatment for installment sales. These tax advantages can enhance the overall financial return for sellers and optimize their after-tax proceeds from the sale.

Beyond the financial benefits, seller financing can also strengthen the relationship between buyers and sellers and facilitate smoother transitions of ownership. By aligning their interests through a mutually beneficial financing arrangement, buyers and sellers can develop a sense of trust and cooperation, fostering a positive and collaborative transaction experience. This alignment of interests can be particularly valuable during the transition period following the sale, as buyers and sellers work together to ensure a seamless transfer of ownership and continuity of operations.

Seller financing is a valuable avenue for facilitating business sales that offers numerous benefits for both buyers and sellers. By providing buyers with access to financing, offering flexible terms and conditions, generating additional income streams for sellers, and providing potential tax advantages, seller financing can enhance the transaction process and create value for all parties involved. Whether it's expanding the pool of potential buyers, optimizing financial returns, or strengthening relationships, seller financing offers a versatile and effective financing solution for businesses seeking to achieve their strategic objectives and maximize their outcomes in the marketplace

The Small Business Administration (SBA) serves as a vital resource for entrepreneurs and small business owners, offering a range of financing solutions designed to support business acquisitions and stimulate economic growth. Through its government-backed loan programs, the SBA provides entrepreneurs with access to affordable capital, enabling them to pursue acquisitions and realize their entrepreneurial aspirations.

SBA financing is particularly valuable for business acquisitions due to its favorable terms and reduced risk for lenders. Unlike conventional loans, which may require substantial collateral and impose stringent eligibility criteria, SBA loans offer more flexible terms and lower down payment requirements, making them accessible to a broader range of borrowers. Additionally, SBA loans are partially guaranteed by the federal government, reducing the risk for lenders and increasing their willingness to extend credit to qualified applicants.

One of the primary advantages of SBA financing is its ability to help buyers overcome traditional lending barriers and access the capital needed to fund their acquisitions. Many entrepreneurs face challenges securing financing for business acquisitions, particularly if they lack significant personal assets or have limited credit history. SBA loans address these challenges by providing borrowers with access to affordable capital and offering more lenient eligibility requirements, allowing them to pursue opportunities that may have been otherwise out of reach.

Furthermore, SBA financing can be instrumental in enabling entrepreneurs to realize their entrepreneurial aspirations and pursue growth opportunities. Whether it's acquiring an existing business, expanding operations, or launching a new venture, access to capital is essential for fueling growth and achieving strategic objectives. By leveraging SBA financing, entrepreneurs can access the capital needed to fund acquisitions, invest in equipment and inventory, hire employees, and execute their business plans effectively.

In addition to providing capital, SBA financing offers other benefits for borrowers, including longer repayment terms, lower interest rates, and access to valuable resources and support services. SBA loans typically feature longer repayment terms than conventional loans, which can help borrowers manage their cash flow and reduce the financial strain associated with debt repayment. Additionally, SBA loans often carry lower interest rates than alternative financing options, reducing the overall cost of borrowing and enhancing the affordability of capital for borrowers.

Moreover, SBA borrowers have access to a wealth of resources and support services provided by the SBA and its network of lending partners. From business counseling and technical assistance to networking opportunities and educational resources, SBA borrowers can tap into a wide range of resources to help them succeed as entrepreneurs. This comprehensive support ecosystem can be invaluable for borrowers as they navigate the complexities of business ownership and management.

The Small Business Administration offers financing solutions to support business acquisitions through its government-backed loan programs. By providing favorable terms, reduced risk for lenders, and access to affordable capital, SBA financing enables entrepreneurs to overcome traditional lending barriers and realize their entrepreneurial aspirations. Whether it's acquiring an existing business, expanding operations, or launching a new venture, SBA financing serves as a valuable resource for entrepreneurs seeking to achieve their business goals and contribute to economic growth and prosperity.

Financing a deal with retirement funds presents a strategic and innovative option for individuals seeking to leverage their existing assets to pursue entrepreneurial endeavors. By utilizing retirement savings to invest in business opportunities, entrepreneurs can access tax-advantaged funds and unlock a wealth of benefits while maintaining control over their retirement savings.

One popular method for financing business ventures with retirement funds is through Rollovers as Business Startups (ROBS) arrangements. ROBS allows individuals to use funds from their retirement accounts, such as 401(k) or IRA accounts, to finance business acquisitions or expansions without incurring early withdrawal penalties or tax liabilities. Instead of withdrawing funds from their retirement accounts, which could trigger taxes and penalties, individuals can roll over their retirement savings into a new business entity, effectively converting their retirement assets into capital for their entrepreneurial endeavors.

One of the primary advantages of financing a deal with retirement funds is the ability to access tax-advantaged funds. Funds held in retirement accounts are typically sheltered from taxes until withdrawn, allowing individuals to invest pre-tax dollars in their businesses and defer taxes on any investment returns or profits generated. By leveraging retirement funds in this manner, entrepreneurs can maximize their investment capital and minimize their tax liabilities, providing a significant financial advantage as they pursue their business objectives.

Furthermore, financing a deal with retirement funds allows individuals to maintain control over their retirement savings while simultaneously investing in their entrepreneurial aspirations. Unlike traditional financing options that may require personal guarantees or collateral, financing with retirement funds allows individuals to access capital without risking their personal assets or creditworthiness. This autonomy and control over retirement savings provide entrepreneurs with the freedom to pursue business opportunities on their terms and execute their vision without outside interference.

Additionally, financing a deal with retirement funds can offer entrepreneurs greater flexibility and agility in pursuing business opportunities. Unlike traditional lenders or investors who may impose strict terms and conditions on financing arrangements, individuals financing with retirement funds have the flexibility to structure deals on their own terms and negotiate favorable terms with sellers or partners. This flexibility can be particularly valuable in competitive markets or fast-moving industries where agility and responsiveness are paramount to success.

Moreover, financing a deal with retirement funds can be a strategic long-term investment strategy, providing individuals with the opportunity to grow their retirement savings through their entrepreneurial endeavors. By investing retirement funds in a business, individuals have the potential to generate significant returns on their investment, which can then be reinvested or rolled back into their retirement accounts to further grow their nest egg. This integrated approach to retirement planning allows individuals to align their business goals with their long-term financial objectives and create wealth over time.

Financing a deal with retirement funds offers individuals a strategic and tax-efficient option for investing in business opportunities. Through vehicles such as ROBS arrangements, entrepreneurs can access tax-advantaged funds from their retirement accounts to finance business acquisitions or expansions while maintaining control over their retirement savings. This approach provides individuals with the flexibility, autonomy, and potential for long-term growth needed to pursue their entrepreneurial aspirations and achieve financial success.

Partnering with a private equity (PE) firm represents a strategic opportunity for businesses seeking to fuel growth and expansion initiatives. Private equity firms specialize in investing in promising businesses with significant growth potential, providing access to substantial capital resources, strategic expertise, and invaluable industry connections. By partnering with a private equity firm, businesses can unlock a myriad of benefits that can accelerate their growth trajectory and enhance their competitive position in the marketplace.

One of the primary advantages of partnering with a private equity firm is access to substantial capital resources. Private equity firms typically manage large pools of capital from institutional investors, high-net-worth individuals, and pension funds, allowing them to provide significant capital injections to support business growth and expansion initiatives. Whether it's funding organic growth initiatives, financing strategic acquisitions, or optimizing operational efficiency, private equity funding can provide businesses with the financial resources needed to execute their growth strategies effectively and achieve their business objectives.

In addition to financial resources, partnering with a private equity firm offers businesses access to strategic expertise and operational guidance. Private equity firms often have seasoned investment professionals with extensive experience in various industries, as well as access to a network of industry experts and advisors. By leveraging this expertise, private equity-backed businesses can gain valuable insights, best practices, and strategic advice to optimize their operations, streamline processes, and capitalize on growth opportunities. Furthermore, private equity firms typically take an active role in the management and governance of their portfolio companies, providing hands-on support and guidance to help businesses achieve their full potential.

Moreover, partnering with a private equity firm can provide businesses with access to invaluable industry connections and networks. Private equity firms often have deep-rooted relationships with key industry players, including suppliers, customers, partners, and potential acquirers. By tapping into these networks, private equity-backed businesses can gain access to new markets, forge strategic partnerships, and identify potential growth opportunities that may otherwise be out of reach. Furthermore, private equity firms can help businesses navigate complex regulatory environments, explore international expansion opportunities, and overcome market challenges by leveraging their extensive industry knowledge and connections.

Furthermore, partnering with a private equity firm can help businesses accelerate their growth trajectory and enhance their competitive position in the marketplace. Private equity-backed businesses often benefit from access to additional resources, expertise, and support that can drive innovation, foster organic growth, and expand market presence. Additionally, private equity firms typically have a long-term investment horizon, allowing businesses to pursue strategic initiatives and investments with a focus on sustainable, long-term value creation. By partnering with a private equity firm, businesses can position themselves for continued growth, success, and profitability in an increasingly competitive business environment.

Partnering with a private equity firm offers businesses access to substantial capital resources, strategic expertise, and invaluable industry connections to support growth and expansion initiatives. By leveraging private equity funding, businesses can access the financial resources needed to execute their growth strategies effectively, gain access to strategic guidance and operational support, and enhance their competitive position in the marketplace. Ultimately, partnering with a private equity firm can provide businesses with the resources, expertise, and support needed to accelerate their growth trajectory and achieve their full potential in the ever-evolving business landscape.

Pitching an innovative acquisition plan to a venture capital (VC) firm can be a game-changing strategy for businesses seeking to expand their products or services. VC firms specialize in financing high-growth startups and innovative ventures, making them ideal partners for companies looking to fuel expansion and rapidly scale operations. By articulating a compelling business case and demonstrating growth potential, entrepreneurs can attract VC investment to execute strategic acquisitions and capitalize on market opportunities.

One of the primary advantages of pitching an acquisition plan to a VC firm is access to substantial capital resources. VC firms manage large pools of capital from institutional investors, endowments, and high-net-worth individuals, specifically earmarked for financing innovative startups and growth-stage companies. By presenting a well-thought-out acquisition plan, entrepreneurs can tap into these capital resources to fund strategic acquisitions, consolidate market share, and accelerate growth initiatives.

Furthermore, VC firms bring more than just financial capital to the table; they also provide strategic guidance, industry expertise, and valuable connections. VC investors often have deep industry knowledge and experience, allowing them to provide valuable insights, strategic advice, and operational support to portfolio companies. By leveraging the expertise and networks of VC investors, entrepreneurs can enhance their acquisition strategies, identify synergies, and navigate complex market dynamics more effectively.

Moreover, VC firms have a vested interest in supporting the growth and success of their portfolio companies, as their returns are tied to the company's performance and valuation. As such, VC investors are typically more willing to take calculated risks and invest in ambitious growth initiatives, including strategic acquisitions. By presenting a compelling business case and demonstrating the potential for value creation, entrepreneurs can attract VC investment to execute strategic acquisitions and capitalize on market opportunities.

In addition to providing capital and strategic support, VC investment can also enhance the credibility and visibility of a company in the marketplace. By securing investment from a reputable VC firm, entrepreneurs can signal to customers, partners, and other stakeholders that their company is well-positioned for growth and success. This increased credibility can open doors to new business opportunities, partnerships, and collaborations, further fueling the company's expansion efforts.

Furthermore, VC investment can help companies overcome financing barriers and achieve economies of scale more rapidly. Strategic acquisitions can provide companies with access to new markets, technologies, and talent, allowing them to expand their product offerings, enhance their competitive position, and capture market share more quickly. By leveraging VC investment to execute strategic acquisitions, entrepreneurs can accelerate their growth trajectory and create long-term value for shareholders.

Pitching an innovative acquisition plan to a venture capital firm can open doors to funding opportunities for expanding products or services. By tapping into the substantial capital resources, strategic guidance, and industry expertise of VC investors, entrepreneurs can fund strategic acquisitions, accelerate growth initiatives, and capitalize on market opportunities. By presenting a compelling business case and demonstrating growth potential, entrepreneurs can attract VC investment to execute strategic acquisitions and drive long-term value creation for their companies and shareholders.s.

Franchising has emerged as a popular growth strategy for entrepreneurs seeking to expand their business footprint while leveraging established brand recognition and proven business models. However, financing the acquisition and expansion of franchises can pose significant challenges for aspiring franchisees. Fortunately, various financing options are available to support franchise acquisitions and expansions, providing entrepreneurs with the capital needed to launch successful ventures within established brand frameworks.

One of the primary financing options available to franchisees is conventional bank loans. Many banks and financial institutions offer loans specifically tailored for franchise businesses, providing aspiring franchisees with access to capital to fund franchise acquisitions, build out locations, and cover operational expenses. Conventional bank loans typically require a solid credit history, collateral, and a well-developed business plan, but they offer competitive interest rates and flexible repayment terms, making them an attractive option for franchise financing. Another financing option for franchisees is Small Business Administration (SBA) loans specifically tailored for franchise businesses. The SBA offers various loan programs designed to support small businesses, including franchise businesses, by providing access to affordable capital and favorable loan terms. SBA loans can be used to finance franchise acquisitions, purchase equipment and inventory, and cover working capital needs. These loans are guaranteed by the SBA, reducing the risk for lenders and making them more accessible to franchisees who may not qualify for traditional bank loans.

Additionally, many franchisors offer financing programs to support franchisees in launching and growing their businesses. These financing programs may include equipment leasing arrangements, vendor financing agreements, or even direct financing from the franchisor itself. By leveraging financing options offered by franchisors, franchisees can access capital tailored to their specific franchise opportunity, often with more favorable terms and fewer barriers to entry.

Regardless of the financing option chosen, franchise financing provides aspiring franchisees with the capital needed to invest in franchise opportunities and launch successful ventures within established brand frameworks. By securing financing, franchisees can overcome financial barriers and pursue their entrepreneurial aspirations with confidence. Furthermore, franchise financing allows entrepreneurs to leverage the proven business models, support systems, and brand recognition offered by franchisors, increasing the likelihood of success and mitigating risks associated with starting a new business from scratch.

Various financing options are available to support franchise acquisitions and expansions, providing aspiring franchisees with access to capital to launch successful ventures within established brand frameworks. Whether through conventional bank loans, SBA loans tailored for franchise businesses, or financing programs offered by franchisors, franchise financing enables entrepreneurs to overcome financial barriers and pursue their entrepreneurial aspirations with confidence. By leveraging financing options, franchisees can tap into the lucrative world of franchising and build thriving businesses within established brand frameworks. In addition to the various financing options available, entrepreneurs considering franchising as a growth strategy can benefit from leveraging the expertise and resources of professionals like Arlind, who have extensive experience and networks within the franchise industry. Arlind, with his network of over 500 different franchises, can provide invaluable support and guidance to aspiring franchisees seeking financing for their ventures. With his deep knowledge of the franchise landscape, Arlind can help entrepreneurs identify suitable franchise opportunities that align with their interests, skills, and financial resources. By leveraging his extensive network of franchisors, Arlind can connect aspiring franchisees with reputable franchise brands that offer financing options tailored to their needs and preferences. Arlind can provide valuable insights and advice on navigating the franchise financing process, helping entrepreneurs understand the various financing options available and determine the most appropriate financing strategy for their specific circumstances. Whether it's evaluating loan terms, negotiating financing agreements, or preparing financing applications, Arlind can provide expert guidance to help entrepreneurs make informed decisions and secure the capital needed to launch their franchise ventures successfully. Arlinds network of over 500 different franchises can provide entrepreneurs with access to a diverse range of financing options and franchising opportunities. By tapping into Adam's extensive network, entrepreneurs can explore a wide array of franchise brands and financing programs, increasing their chances of finding the perfect fit for their business goals and objectives. Arlind's expertise and network within the franchise industry can be instrumental in helping entrepreneurs secure financing for their franchise ventures. By leveraging his knowledge, experience, and extensive network of franchisors, Adam can provide aspiring franchisees with access to a wealth of financing options and franchising opportunities, increasing their chances of success in the competitive world of franchising. With Arlind's support and guidance, entrepreneurs can navigate the franchise financing process with confidence and launch successful franchise ventures within established brand frameworks. Financing is a fundamental enabler of business transactions and growth initiatives, offering entrepreneurs a range of options to access capital and realize their strategic objectives. Whether through all-cash transactions, seller financing, government-backed programs, retirement fund utilization, private equity partnerships, venture capital investments, or franchise financing, businesses can leverage diverse financing sources to fuel expansion, acquisitions, and entrepreneurial endeavors. By exploring and leveraging these financing options strategically, entrepreneurs can unlock new opportunities for growth and success in the competitive business landscape.

Chapter 4: The Team

Building the right team is essential for navigating the complex landscape of mergers and acquisitions (M&A). Whether you're a seasoned entrepreneur or new to the world of M&A, assembling a team of experienced professionals can make all the difference in achieving successful outcomes. In this chapter, we'll explore the key roles of M&A advisors, lawyers, accountants, and other specialists, as well as tips for hiring and working with them effectively.

Mergers and acquisitions (M&A) represent complex and high-stakes endeavors for businesses seeking growth, consolidation, or strategic repositioning within their industries. In this landscape of intricate deal structures, regulatory landscapes, and financial intricacies, M&A advisors emerge as indispensable allies, guiding businesses through every step of the process with strategic acumen and expert insight.

First and foremost, M&A advisors serve as the vanguards of strategic navigation, guiding businesses through the labyrinthine intricacies of the M&A process. Armed with a wealth of experience and industry knowledge, these professionals offer invaluable strategic advice that helps businesses identify opportunities, evaluate potential targets, and navigate the myriad complexities of deal-making. By understanding the unique objectives and challenges of their clients, M&A advisors craft tailored strategies that align with their clients' long-term goals and maximize value creation.

Moreover, M&A advisors provide indispensable market insights that enable businesses to make informed decisions and stay ahead of emerging trends and competitive dynamics. Through rigorous market analysis and due diligence, M&A advisors identify opportunities and risks, assess market conditions, and provide actionable intelligence that informs strategic decision-making. By leveraging their deep understanding of industry dynamics and market trends, M&A advisors help businesses seize opportunities and capitalize on favorable market conditions while mitigating risks and challenges.

Transactional expertise is another hallmark of M&A advisors, who possess the specialized knowledge and skills needed to navigate the intricacies of deal structuring, negotiation, and execution. From conducting financial valuations and modeling complex financial scenarios to drafting transaction documents and negotiating deal terms, M&A advisors play a pivotal role in facilitating successful transactions from inception to closing. Their expertise in deal structuring and negotiation ensures that their clients achieve favorable outcomes and secure the best possible terms while mitigating risks and protecting their interests.

M&A advisors act as trusted partners and confidants, building relationships of trust and confidence with their clients. By serving as trusted advisors, M&A professionals earn the trust and respect of their clients, who rely on their guidance and expertise to navigate the complexities of the M&A process. M&A advisors prioritize their clients' interests above all else, working tirelessly to maximize value and minimize risks while fostering open communication and collaboration throughout the entire transaction lifecycle.

M&A advisors play a crucial role in guiding businesses through the intricacies of the M&A process, providing strategic advice, market insights, and transactional expertise that enable their clients to achieve their strategic objectives effectively. By serving as trusted partners and leveraging their industry knowledge and networks, M&A advisors help businesses identify opportunities, evaluate targets, negotiate deals, and navigate regulatory requirements with confidence and clarity. In a landscape of complex deal-making, M&A advisors emerge as indispensable allies, guiding businesses towards success and unlocking value in every transaction..

In the realm of M&A advisory, professionals like Arlind Sadiku serve as linchpins, bridging the gap between businesses and their strategic objectives. Arlind, as an M&A advisor, embodies the quintessential role of a trusted partner, offering personalized guidance, strategic foresight, and unparalleled expertise to businesses navigating the complexities of mergers and acquisitions.

Arlind's role as an M&A advisor extends far beyond providing strategic advice and transactional expertise; he acts as a catalyst for success, leveraging his industry knowledge and extensive network to drive value creation and mitigate risks for his clients. With a keen understanding of his clients' objectives, Arlind crafts tailored strategies that align with their long-term goals, helping businesses identify opportunities, evaluate targets, and execute transactions that maximize value.

Arlind's deep-rooted connections within the industry provide businesses with access to a vast network of potential buyers, sellers, investors, and strategic partners. By leveraging his extensive network, Arlind facilitates meaningful connections and fosters collaboration, enabling businesses to explore new opportunities, forge strategic alliances, and unlock growth potential.

Arlind's transactional expertise and deal-making prowess are instrumental in guiding businesses through every stage of the M&A process. From conducting thorough due diligence and financial analysis to structuring transactions and negotiating deal terms, Arlind ensures that his clients achieve favorable outcomes and secure the best possible terms while mitigating risks and protecting their interests.

Arlind's role as an M&A advisor extends beyond transactional support; he serves as a trusted advisor and confidant, building relationships of trust and confidence with his clients. By prioritizing open communication, transparency, and collaboration, Arlind fosters a collaborative partnership with his clients, empowering them to make informed decisions and navigate the complexities of the M&A process with clarity and confidence.

Arlind's role as an M&A advisor is multifaceted and invaluable, encompassing strategic guidance, transactional expertise, and trusted partnership. Through personalized advice, strategic foresight, and unparalleled industry knowledge, Arlind empowers businesses to achieve their strategic objectives effectively and unlock value in every transaction. As a trusted advisor and confidant, Arlind serves as a linchpin, bridging the gap between businesses and their aspirations, and driving success in the dynamic landscape of mergers and acquisitions.

In the intricate world of mergers and acquisitions (M&A), lawyers play a pivotal role as indispensable members of the M&A team, offering crucial legal expertise and ensuring compliance with the myriad laws and regulations governing such transactions. M&A lawyers are essential in every stage of the M&A process, from initial negotiations to final closing, providing invaluable guidance and support to their clients.

One of the primary roles of M&A lawyers is to help structure transactions in a manner that maximizes value and minimizes risks for their clients. Drawing on their expertise in corporate law and transactional matters, M&A lawyers work closely with their clients to develop transaction structures that align with their strategic objectives and mitigate potential legal and financial risks. By crafting well-designed transaction structures, M&A lawyers help their clients achieve their desired outcomes while safeguarding their interests.

M&A lawyers are responsible for drafting and reviewing the legal documents that govern M&A transactions, including purchase agreements, merger agreements, and disclosure documents. These legal documents are complex and intricate, requiring meticulous attention to detail and a deep understanding of legal principles and contractual obligations. M&A lawyers ensure that these documents accurately reflect the terms and conditions of the transaction, protect their clients' rights and interests, and comply with applicable laws and regulations.

M&A lawyers play a critical role in negotiating the terms of M&A transactions on behalf of their clients. Whether negotiating purchase price adjustments, indemnification provisions, or representations and warranties, M&A lawyers leverage their negotiation skills and legal expertise to secure favorable terms for their clients. By advocating for their clients' interests and protecting them from potential liabilities, M&A lawyers help ensure that their clients achieve successful outcomes in M&A transactions.

M&A lawyers are instrumental in mitigating legal risks associated with M&A activities. They conduct comprehensive due diligence reviews to identify potential legal issues and liabilities, such as contractual breaches, regulatory violations, and litigation risks. By identifying these risks early in the process, M&A lawyers enable their clients to make informed decisions and take appropriate measures to mitigate or address them effectively.

M&A lawyers are experts in regulatory compliance, ensuring that M&A transactions comply with the relevant laws and regulations governing corporate transactions. They navigate complex regulatory frameworks, such as antitrust laws, securities regulations, and tax laws, to ensure that transactions are executed in compliance with applicable legal requirements. By staying abreast of changes in the regulatory landscape and advising their clients accordingly, M&A lawyers help mitigate regulatory risks and facilitate smooth and successful transactions.

M&A lawyers are indispensable members of Arlinds M&A team, providing legal expertise and ensuring compliance with relevant laws and regulations throughout the transaction process. From structuring transactions and drafting legal documents to negotiating terms and mitigating legal risks, M&A lawyers play a critical role in safeguarding the interests of their clients and facilitating successful M&A transactions. Their expertise in corporate law, contract negotiation, and regulatory compliance is essential for navigating the complexities of M&A transactions and achieving favorable outcomes for their clients.

In the intricate landscape of mergers and acquisitions (M&A), accountants emerge as critical players, offering invaluable financial expertise and analysis that are essential for navigating the complexities of the M&A process. With their specialized skills in financial analysis, due diligence, and valuation, M&A accountants play a pivotal role in assessing the financial health and value of target companies, identifying potential risks and opportunities, and optimizing deal structures to maximize value for their clients.

One of the primary roles of M&A accountants is to conduct thorough financial analysis of target companies, evaluating their financial performance, profitability, and solvency. Through rigorous financial analysis, M&A accountants assess key financial metrics, such as revenue growth, profit margins, cash flow, and liquidity, to gain insights into the financial health and viability of target companies. By analyzing financial data and identifying trends and patterns, M&A accountants provide valuable insights that inform strategic decisions and help their clients assess the potential risks and opportunities associated with M&A transactions.

Moreover, M&A accountants play a crucial role in conducting due diligence, a comprehensive review of the target company's financial and operational performance. Through due diligence, M&A accountants examine financial statements, tax returns, contracts, and other relevant documents to assess the accuracy and completeness of financial information, identify potential risks and liabilities, and uncover any hidden issues that may impact the transaction. By conducting due diligence, M&A accountants help their clients make informed decisions and mitigate risks associated with M&A transactions.

Additionally, M&A accountants provide valuation services to determine the fair market value of target companies and assets. Using a variety of valuation methods, such as discounted cash flow analysis, comparable company analysis, and precedent transactions analysis, M&A accountants assess the intrinsic value of target companies and assets, taking into account factors such as growth prospects, market conditions, and industry dynamics. By providing accurate and reliable valuations, M&A accountants enable their clients to negotiate favorable deal terms and maximize value in M&A transactions.

Furthermore, M&A accountants ensure transparency and accuracy in financial reporting, helping to maintain the integrity and credibility of financial information throughout the M&A process. By conducting financial audits and reviews, M&A accountants verify the accuracy and completeness of financial statements, identify any discrepancies or irregularities, and ensure compliance with accounting standards and regulatory requirements. Their expertise in financial reporting and accounting principles is essential for maintaining investor confidence and facilitating successful M&A transactions. Arlinds M&A accountants team play a critical role in the M&A process, providing financial analysis, due diligence, and valuation services that are essential for assessing the financial health and value of target companies. Through their insights and analysis, M&A accountants help identify potential risks and opportunities, inform strategic decisions, and optimize deal structures to maximize value for their clients. Their expertise in financial reporting and accounting principles ensures transparency and accuracy in financial information, maintaining the integrity of M&A transactions and facilitating successful outcomes for their clients. When hiring and working with M&A advisors, lawyers, accountants, and other specialists, there are several tips to keep in mind. First, it's essential to choose professionals with relevant experience and expertise in M&A transactions and the specific industry or market segment in which you operate. Look for professionals who have a track record of success and a deep understanding of the nuances of M&A negotiations and deal-making. Communication is also key when working with advisors and specialists. Establish clear expectations, goals, and timelines upfront, and maintain open and transparent communication throughout the process. Regular updates, status reports, and meetings can help ensure alignment and keep everyone on the same page. Furthermore, it's essential to foster a collaborative and cohesive team dynamic among advisors and specialists. Encourage teamwork, mutual respect, and information sharing to leverage the collective expertise and insights of the team. By working together effectively, advisors and specialists can identify opportunities, address challenges, and drive successful outcomes for their clients. In addition to M&A advisors, lawyers, and accountants, there may be other specialists or experts whose expertise is needed to support specific aspects of the M&A process. These specialists may include tax advisors, valuation experts, industry consultants, or regulatory experts, depending on the nature of the transaction and the unique needs of the parties involved. By assembling a multidisciplinary team of professionals with complementary skills and expertise, businesses can navigate the complexities of M&A transactions with confidence and achieve their strategic objectives effectively. Building the right team is essential for success in M&A transactions. M&A advisors, lawyers, accountants, and other specialists play critical roles in guiding businesses through the intricacies of the M&A process and facilitating successful outcomes. By hiring experienced professionals, fostering open communication and collaboration, and leveraging the expertise of a multidisciplinary team, businesses can navigate M&A transactions with confidence and achieve their strategic objectives effectively.

Chapter 5: Meet The Buyers

In the dynamic world of mergers and acquisitions (M&A), understanding the various types of buyers is essential for navigating the complexities of the deal-making landscape. Buyers come in various forms, each with distinct motivations, strategies, and objectives. In this chapter, we'll explore the five types of buyers commonly encountered in the M&A arena: individual buyers, financial buyers, strategic buyers, industry buyers, and other buyers.

In the dynamic realm of mergers and acquisitions (M&A), individual buyers stand out as a unique and diverse category, comprising high-net-worth individuals and entrepreneurs who bring a personal touch to the deal-making landscape. Driven by a myriad of motivations and objectives, individual buyers play a significant role in the M&A market, leveraging their expertise, experience, and resources to pursue strategic opportunities and drive value creation.

Individual buyers often come from diverse backgrounds, ranging from seasoned investors and serial entrepreneurs to industry professionals and executives looking to make strategic investments. These buyers are typically motivated by a desire to diversify their investment portfolios, seeking opportunities to allocate capital across a range of asset classes and industries. By acquiring businesses, individual buyers can achieve greater diversification and reduce exposure to market risks, enhancing the resilience and stability of their investment portfolios.

Individual buyers may be driven by a desire to pursue entrepreneurial opportunities and take an active role in shaping the future direction of acquired businesses. For many entrepreneurs, M&A presents a unique opportunity to leverage their skills, experience, and vision to build and grow successful businesses. By acquiring existing businesses, individual buyers can capitalize on synergies, economies of scale, and operational efficiencies to drive growth and maximize returns on their investments.

Additionally, individual buyers often bring a hands-on approach to M&A transactions, leveraging their expertise and experience to add value and achieve their strategic objectives. Unlike institutional investors or corporate buyers, individual buyers have the flexibility to take a more personal and involved approach to managing acquired businesses, implementing strategic initiatives, and driving operational improvements. This hands-on approach allows individual buyers to align the interests of stakeholders, foster a culture of innovation, and capitalize on growth opportunities more effectively.

Individual buyers may seek to capitalize on synergies with existing businesses or investment holdings, leveraging their industry knowledge, networks, and resources to create value through strategic acquisitions. By acquiring businesses that complement their existing operations or fill gaps in their product portfolios, individual buyers can achieve greater strategic alignment and enhance the overall competitiveness and profitability of their enterprises.

Individual buyers represent a unique category of buyers in the M&A landscape, bringing a personal touch and entrepreneurial spirit to the deal-making process. Motivated by a desire to diversify their investment portfolios, pursue entrepreneurial opportunities, or capitalize on synergies with existing businesses, individual buyers play a significant role in driving value creation and achieving strategic objectives through M&A transactions. With their hands-on approach, expertise, and experience, individual buyers are well-positioned to navigate the complexities of the M&A market and unlock opportunities for growth and success in an ever-evolving business landscape.

Financial buyers, commonly known as private equity firms or investment groups, are key players in the vibrant landscape of mergers and acquisitions (M&A). Distinguished by their strategic focus on generating attractive returns for their investors, financial buyers wield significant influence in the M&A market, specializing in the acquisition of businesses poised for growth and value creation.

At the heart of their strategy, financial buyers prioritize the acquisition of businesses with strong growth potential, stable cash flows, and opportunities for operational improvements or expansion. By targeting businesses with these characteristics, financial buyers aim to capitalize on the intrinsic value and growth opportunities inherent in their target companies, thereby maximizing returns for their investors over the investment horizon.

Central to the modus operandi of financial buyers is the utilization of leveraged buyout (LBO) strategies to finance acquisitions. Leveraging a combination of equity and debt financing, financial buyers structure transactions in a manner that optimizes returns while minimizing capital requirements. By leveraging debt, financial buyers can amplify their returns on equity investment, thereby enhancing the overall profitability of their investments.

Financial buyers are adept at identifying and executing operational improvements and growth initiatives post-acquisition. Leveraging their extensive networks, industry expertise, and operational capabilities, financial buyers work closely with management teams to implement value-enhancing strategies, streamline operations, and drive growth. Whether through organic growth initiatives, strategic acquisitions, or operational efficiencies, financial buyers are committed to maximizing the value and profitability of their portfolio companies.

In addition to their focus on operational improvements, financial buyers are also skilled at identifying and executing add-on acquisitions to further enhance the value of their portfolio companies. By leveraging their industry knowledge and network of contacts, financial buyers identify strategic acquisition targets that complement the existing operations of their portfolio companies, thereby creating synergies and unlocking additional value.

Moreover, financial buyers play a crucial role in providing liquidity and exit opportunities for business owners and entrepreneurs looking to monetize their investments. By acquiring businesses and facilitating liquidity events, financial buyers enable business owners to realize the value of their investments while providing a pathway for continued growth and success under new ownership.

Financial buyers, including private equity firms and investment groups, are prominent players in the M&A market, specializing in the acquisition of businesses with strong growth potential and opportunities for value creation. By employing leveraged buyout strategies, driving operational improvements, and executing strategic acquisitions, financial buyers generate attractive returns for their investors while providing liquidity and exit opportunities for business owners. With their focus on maximizing value and driving growth, financial buyers play a pivotal role in shaping the landscape of mergers and acquisitions.

In the dynamic landscape of mergers and acquisitions (M&A), strategic buyers emerge as pivotal players, driven by a distinct set of motivations and objectives that differentiate them from other categories of buyers. Unlike financial buyers who prioritize generating attractive returns for their investors, strategic buyers are companies seeking to acquire other businesses as part of their growth or expansion strategies, with a keen focus on achieving strategic objectives and creating long-term value.

At the core of their strategy, strategic buyers are motivated by a desire to enhance their competitive positioning and drive growth through acquisitions. These buyers may seek to enter new markets, expand product offerings, diversify revenue streams, or achieve operational synergies by acquiring complementary businesses. By identifying strategic acquisition targets that align with their long-term objectives, strategic buyers aim to capitalize on synergies and unlock value that enhances their overall competitive advantage and profitability.

One of the primary motivations driving strategic buyers is the opportunity to fill gaps in their product portfolios or consolidate market share within their industries. By acquiring businesses with complementary products, technologies, or customer bases, strategic buyers can strengthen their market position, expand their product offerings, and capture a larger share of the market. Additionally, strategic buyers may leverage acquisitions to gain access to new technologies, intellectual property, or distribution channels that enable them to differentiate their products and services and drive innovation.

Moreover, strategic buyers often prioritize achieving operational synergies through acquisitions, seeking to streamline operations, reduce costs, and improve efficiency across their organizations. By integrating acquired businesses into their existing operations and leveraging shared resources and capabilities, strategic buyers can achieve economies of scale and drive operational efficiencies that enhance profitability and competitiveness. This focus on operational synergies allows strategic buyers to maximize the value of their acquisitions and achieve sustainable growth over the long term.

Furthermore, strategic buyers are often willing to pay a premium for synergistic acquisitions that align with their long-term strategic objectives. Unlike financial buyers who may prioritize valuation metrics and investment returns, strategic buyers place a premium on strategic fit and alignment with their core business objectives. As such, they may be willing to pay a higher price for acquisitions that offer significant strategic value and growth opportunities, even if it means accepting a lower short-term return on investment.

Strategic buyers play a pivotal role in the M&A market, driven by a strategic rationale for acquisitions that prioritizes long-term value creation and competitive advantage. By seeking to enter new markets, expand product offerings, diversify revenue streams, or achieve operational synergies, strategic buyers aim to enhance their competitive positioning and drive growth through strategic acquisitions. With their focus on strategic fit and long-term objectives, strategic buyers contribute to the dynamism and evolution of the M&A landscape, shaping the future of industries and driving innovation and growth.

In the vibrant arena of mergers and acquisitions (M&A), industry buyers stand out as formidable players, possessing a unique advantage born from their intimate knowledge and deep-rooted connections within their respective industries or sectors. These buyers, operating within the same industry or sector as the target company, leverage their unparalleled understanding of industry dynamics, market trends, and competitive landscapes to capitalize on synergies and unlock value through strategic acquisitions.

At the core of their strategy, industry buyers harness their insider knowledge and industry expertise to identify strategic acquisition targets that align with their long-term objectives and complement their existing operations. Armed with a deep understanding of industry trends, market dynamics, and competitive pressures, industry buyers are well-positioned to identify opportunities for growth and value creation that may not be apparent to outsiders.

One of the key advantages of industry buyers lies in their ability to capitalize on synergies through strategic acquisitions. By acquiring businesses within their industry or sector, industry buyers can leverage shared resources, capabilities, and customer bases to drive operational efficiencies and unlock value. Whether through economies of scale, cross-selling opportunities, or shared distribution channels, industry buyers can achieve significant cost savings and revenue enhancements that enhance their competitive positioning and profitability.

Moreover, industry buyers may seek to consolidate market share within their industry or sector through strategic acquisitions. By acquiring competitors or complementary businesses, industry buyers can strengthen their market position, expand their customer base, and increase their market share, thereby enhancing their competitive advantage and driving growth. Additionally, industry buyers may use acquisitions to expand their geographic presence or gain access to new markets, enabling them to capitalize on growth opportunities and diversify their revenue streams.

Furthermore, industry buyers may pursue acquisitions to gain access to complementary technologies or capabilities that enhance their product offerings or competitive differentiation. Whether acquiring companies with proprietary technologies, intellectual property, or specialized expertise, industry buyers can strengthen their product portfolios and innovation capabilities, positioning themselves for long-term success in rapidly evolving industries.

Industry buyers play a pivotal role in the M&A landscape, leveraging their deep industry knowledge and expertise to identify and execute strategic acquisitions that drive value and enhance competitive positioning. By capitalizing on synergies, consolidating market share, expanding geographic presence, and gaining access to complementary technologies or capabilities, industry buyers unlock growth opportunities and create value for their stakeholders. With their insider perspective and strategic vision, industry buyers shape the future of their industries, driving innovation, growth, and resilience in dynamic and competitive markets. In the dynamic world of mergers and acquisitions (M&A), the category of "other buyers" encompasses a diverse array of entities that defy easy categorization but nonetheless wield significant influence in the M&A market. These buyers, which include family offices, sovereign wealth funds, conglomerates, and foreign investors, among others, contribute to the richness and complexity of the M&A landscape, bringing unique perspectives, resources, and opportunities to the table. Family offices represent one segment of other buyers, comprising private investment vehicles established to manage the wealth and assets of affluent families. With substantial financial resources at their disposal, family offices often pursue M&A opportunities as part of their investment strategies, seeking to diversify their portfolios, generate attractive returns, and preserve wealth across generations. Family offices may have a long-term investment horizon and a more flexible approach to deal-making, enabling them to capitalize on unique opportunities that align with their investment objectives and risk tolerance.

Sovereign wealth funds, on the other hand, are state-owned investment funds that manage and invest government-owned assets. These funds, typically established by resource-rich countries or governments with significant financial reserves, play a prominent role in the global M&A market, deploying capital to pursue strategic investments and generate returns for their stakeholders. Sovereign wealth funds may invest in a wide range of sectors and geographies, seeking opportunities that align with their strategic objectives, risk appetite, and investment mandates. Conglomerates represent another category of other buyers, comprising diversified corporations with interests in multiple industries or sectors. These buyers may pursue M&A opportunities to expand their business portfolios, diversify revenue streams, and capitalize on synergies across their various business units. Conglomerates may have the financial resources, operational expertise, and market knowledge to pursue strategic acquisitions that enhance their competitive positioning and drive long-term growth and profitability. Foreign investors looking to establish residency in the country, can take advantage by attracting government incentives of investing and obtaining residency including multinational corporations and international investment funds, also play a significant role in the M&A market as other buyers. These investors may seek opportunities to expand their presence in new markets, gain access to strategic assets or technologies, or diversify their geographic footprint through cross-border acquisitions. Foreign investors bring diverse perspectives, expertise, and resources to the table, contributing to the globalization and interconnectedness of the M&A landscape.

While the motivations and strategies of other buyers may vary widely, they all contribute to the diversity and dynamism of the M&A market, bringing unique perspectives and opportunities to the table. Whether family offices, sovereign wealth funds, conglomerates, or foreign investors, these buyers enrich the M&A landscape with their financial resources, strategic vision, and willingness to explore new opportunities. In an ever-evolving business environment, the presence of other buyers ensures that the M&A market remains vibrant, innovative, and responsive to changing market dynamics and opportunities.

A company may also acquire another business for a multitude of reasons, each driven by strategic objectives aimed at enhancing its competitive position, driving growth, or creating value for stakeholders. Below are some of the key motivations behind why a company may choose to pursue an acquisition: Strategic Expansion: Acquisitions provide companies with opportunities to expand their market presence, geographic footprint, or product/service offerings strategically. By acquiring businesses operating in complementary markets or industries, companies can access new customer segments, distribution channels, or technologies, thereby accelerating their growth trajectory and enhancing their competitive advantage.

Market Consolidation: In competitive industries, companies may pursue acquisitions as a means of consolidating market share and solidifying their position as industry leaders. By acquiring competitors or complementary businesses, companies can eliminate competition, achieve economies of scale, and strengthen their market position, enabling them to command greater pricing power and profitability.

Diversification: Acquisitions offer companies opportunities to diversify their revenue streams, product portfolios, or customer bases, reducing reliance on a single market or business segment. By acquiring businesses operating in different industries or serving distinct customer segments, companies can mitigate risks associated with market volatility or cyclical downturns, enhancing the stability and resilience of their operations. Synergies: Acquisitions can create synergies that drive operational efficiencies, cost savings, or revenue enhancements for the acquiring company. Synergies may arise from shared resources, complementary capabilities, or economies of scale achieved through the integration of acquired businesses into existing operations. By leveraging synergies, companies can unlock value and improve overall profitability. Access to Talent and Expertise: Acquiring businesses may provide companies with access to specialized talent, expertise, or intellectual property that is critical for driving innovation and sustaining competitive advantage. By integrating talented teams or acquiring proprietary technologies, companies can enhance their innovation capabilities, accelerate product development cycles, and stay ahead of industry trends. Vertical Integration: Companies may pursue vertical integration through acquisitions to gain control over critical inputs, distribution channels, or downstream activities in their value chain. By acquiring suppliers, distributors, or retail outlets, companies can streamline operations, reduce dependency on external partners, and capture greater value along the supply chain. Financial Considerations: Acquisitions may be driven by financial considerations, such as achieving economies of scale, enhancing shareholder value, or generating attractive returns on investment. Companies may pursue acquisitions that offer favorable valuation multiples, accretive earnings potential, or opportunities for value creation through operational improvements or cost efficiencies. Companies may acquire businesses for a variety of strategic, operational, and financial reasons aimed at enhancing their competitive position, driving growth, and creating value for stakeholders. Whether pursuing strategic expansion, market consolidation, diversification, synergies, access to talent, vertical integration, or financial considerations, acquisitions represent a powerful tool for companies to achieve their strategic objectives and fuel long-term success in today's dynamic business environment. Understanding the various types of buyers is essential for navigating the complexities of the M&A market effectively. Whether individual buyers, financial buyers, strategic buyers, industry buyers, or other buyers, each category brings its own set of motivations, strategies, and objectives to M&A transactions. By recognizing the distinct characteristics of each type of buyer, businesses can tailor their M&A strategies and maximize value creation in an ever-evolving marketplace.

Chapter 6: Marketing in M&A

In the realm of mergers and acquisitions (M&A), effective marketing strategies play a crucial role in identifying and engaging potential buyers or investors. This delves into the various approaches to marketing in M&A, including the distinction between fishing and hunting for buyers, leveraging ad portals and targeted campaigns, and other methods for finding buyers. Additionally, it covers essential aspects such as maintaining confidentiality, screening buyers, employees, non-U.S. citizen buyers, investors, and avoiding tire kickers.

In the dynamic world of mergers and acquisitions (M&A), finding the right buyers or investors is a critical aspect of achieving successful outcomes. Two distinct approaches to this process are fishing and hunting, each offering unique strategies for identifying and engaging potential stakeholders in the M&A market.

Fishing represents a passive approach to finding buyers or investors, akin to casting a wide net into a vast ocean of opportunities. In this approach, sellers utilize ad portals, online listings, and other marketing channels to showcase their businesses to a broad audience of potential buyers. Ad portals serve as virtual marketplaces where sellers can create listings that highlight key features, financial metrics, and growth prospects of their businesses.

The primary advantage of fishing is its ability to reach a large and diverse audience of potential buyers, thereby increasing visibility and generating interest in the opportunity. By casting a wide net through ad portals and online listings, sellers can attract a broad range of prospective buyers, including individuals, companies, private equity firms, and other investors who may be interested in acquiring or investing in the business.

Furthermore, fishing allows sellers to passively engage with potential buyers without the need for proactive outreach or targeted marketing campaigns. Sellers can create compelling listings on ad portals and leverage online marketing channels to promote their businesses, attracting attention and inquiries from interested parties without expending significant time or resources on active prospecting efforts.

Ad portals serve as virtual marketplaces where sellers can showcase their businesses to a broad audience of potential buyers, increasing visibility and generating interest.

However, while fishing offers the potential to reach a wide audience, it may also result in a high volume of inquiries from unqualified or unsuitable buyers. Sorting through these inquiries can be time-consuming and may distract sellers from focusing on qualified prospects who are genuinely interested and capable of pursuing the opportunity.

Fishing represents a passive approach to finding buyers or investors in the M&A market, leveraging ad portals, online listings, and other marketing channels to cast a wide net and attract potential stakeholders. While fishing offers the potential to reach a broad audience and generate interest in the opportunity, sellers must be prepared to sift through inquiries and prioritize qualified prospects to ensure a successful outcome. Ultimately, fishing serves as a valuable tool in the M&A toolkit, complementing more proactive approaches such as hunting and targeted marketing campaigns to maximize visibility and engagement in the marketplace.

In the intricate realm of mergers and acquisitions (M&A), hunting emerges as a strategic approach where sellers actively pursue potential buyers or investors through personalized outreach and targeted marketing campaigns. Unlike fishing, which casts a wide net to attract a broad audience, hunting involves a more focused and deliberate effort to identify and engage with qualified stakeholders who align with the seller's objectives and criteria.

At the core of hunting lies a meticulous process of market research, industry analysis, and data-driven insights to identify potential buyers or investors who meet specific criteria and are more likely to be interested in the opportunity. Sellers leverage market intelligence, industry trends, and proprietary databases to identify target segments, understand their preferences and motivations, and tailor their outreach efforts accordingly.

One of the primary advantages of hunting is its ability to target qualified buyers or investors who are genuinely interested and capable of pursuing the opportunity. By focusing on specific criteria such as industry expertise, financial capacity, strategic fit, and acquisition goals, sellers can identify stakeholders who are more likely to see value in the opportunity and engage in meaningful discussions.

Moreover, hunting enables sellers to personalize their outreach efforts and tailor their messaging to resonate with the target audience effectively. By understanding the needs, challenges, and priorities of potential buyers or investors, sellers can craft compelling value propositions that highlight the unique benefits and opportunities associated with the opportunity, increasing the likelihood of engagement and interest.

Hunting allows sellers to maintain control over the process and prioritize qualified prospects over unqualified or unsuitable inquiries. By proactively identifying and engaging with potential stakeholders, sellers can streamline the transaction process, reduce time-to-close, and minimize distractions from unqualified prospects who may not be serious or capable of pursuing the opportunity.

Hunting fosters a strategic and proactive approach to M&A, enabling sellers to drive value creation and achieve their objectives effectively. By actively seeking out qualified buyers or investors who align with their strategic vision and goals, sellers can unlock opportunities for growth, expansion, and value realization that may not be readily available through passive approaches such as fishing.

Hunting represents a targeted and strategic approach to finding buyers or investors in the M&A market, leveraging personalized outreach and targeted marketing campaigns to engage with qualified stakeholders who align with the seller's objectives and criteria. By leveraging market research, industry insights, and proprietary databases, sellers can identify and engage with potential buyers or investors who are genuinely interested and capable of pursuing the opportunity, driving value creation and achieving successful outcomes in the dynamic landscape of mergers and acquisitions.

In the realm of mergers and acquisitions (M&A), finding the right buyers or investors is a critical aspect of achieving successful outcomes. While approaches like fishing and hunting are essential, other methods complement these strategies, enabling sellers to access a broader pool of potential buyers and increase the likelihood of finding the right match for their business. These methods include networking within industry associations, engaging with business brokers or M&A advisors, and tapping into personal or professional networks for referrals and introductions.

Networking within industry associations serves as a valuable avenue for connecting with potential buyers or investors who have a vested interest in the industry or sector. By participating in industry events, conferences, and networking forums, sellers can establish relationships with industry professionals, executives, and decision-makers who may be interested in exploring M&A opportunities. These networking opportunities provide sellers with access to a targeted audience of potential buyers who possess industry expertise, market knowledge, and strategic insights that can enhance the value proposition of their businesses.

Engaging with business brokers or M&A advisors is another effective method for finding buyers or investors in the M&A market. Business brokers and M&A advisors specialize in facilitating transactions between buyers and sellers, leveraging their networks, expertise, and experience to match sellers with qualified buyers or investors. By enlisting the services of a reputable business broker or M&A advisor, sellers can benefit from their market knowledge, negotiation skills, and transactional expertise, increasing the likelihood of achieving successful outcomes in M&A transactions.

Additionally, tapping into personal or professional networks for referrals and introductions can yield valuable connections and opportunities in the M&A market. Sellers can leverage their existing relationships with colleagues, peers, mentors, and industry contacts to identify potential buyers or investors who may be interested in exploring M&A opportunities. By leveraging personal or professional networks, sellers can access a trusted network of contacts who can provide referrals, introductions, and recommendations, facilitating meaningful engagements and discussions with qualified stakeholders.

These methods enable sellers to access a broader pool of potential buyers and increase the likelihood of finding the right match for their business. By networking within industry associations, engaging with business brokers or M&A advisors, and tapping into personal or professional networks for referrals and introductions, sellers can leverage a diverse range of channels and resources to identify and engage with qualified buyers or investors who align with their strategic objectives and criteria. Ultimately, these methods complement fishing and hunting approaches, enhancing sellers' visibility, reach, and effectiveness in the competitive landscape of mergers and acquisitions.

In navigating the intricate landscape of mergers and acquisitions (M&A), having access to a global network of buyers can significantly enhance the effectiveness of finding the right match for a business. Arlind, with his extensive global network of buyers, plays a pivotal role in solving the challenge of identifying potential buyers or investors for M&A transactions.

Arlind's global network encompasses a diverse range of buyers from various industries, sectors, and regions worldwide. Leveraging his connections, relationships, and expertise, Arlind and his team can tap into a vast pool of qualified buyers who are actively seeking M&A opportunities. Whether individuals, companies, private equity firms, or institutional investors, Arlinds's network spans across different buyer categories, enabling sellers to access a broad spectrum of potential stakeholders.

Arlind's global network provides sellers with access to international markets and opportunities beyond their local or regional boundaries. By connecting sellers with buyers from different geographic regions and cultural backgrounds, Arlind facilitates cross-border transactions and opens doors to new growth opportunities and strategic partnerships.

Sellers can benefit from Arlind's insights into global market trends, regulatory landscapes, and cultural nuances, enabling them to navigate the complexities of international M&A transactions with confidence and clarity.

Arlind's global network offers sellers a competitive advantage in identifying and engaging with qualified buyers who possess specific criteria and preferences aligned with their business objectives. By leveraging his market knowledge, industry expertise, and proprietary databases, Arlind can tailor his outreach efforts and target potential buyers who are more likely to be interested and capable of pursuing the opportunity. This targeted approach enhances the efficiency and effectiveness of the buyer identification process, increasing the likelihood of successful outcomes in M&A transactions.

Arlind's global network of buyers serves as a valuable resource for sellers in the M&A market, offering access to a diverse range of qualified buyers, international markets, and strategic opportunities. By leveraging his connections, relationships, and expertise, Arlind facilitates meaningful engagements and discussions between sellers and buyers, driving value creation and achieving successful outcomes in the dynamic landscape of mergers and acquisitions. With Arlind's global network, sellers can navigate the complexities of the M&A process with confidence, knowing that they have access to the right buyers who can unlock the full potential of their businesses on a global scale.

Maintaining confidentiality is a cornerstone of successful mergers and acquisitions (M&A) transactions, as it protects sensitive information and prevents disruptions to the business. In this essay, we'll explore why confidentiality is paramount in M&A, the role of Non-Disclosure Agreements (NDAs) in safeguarding confidential information, and the importance of preparing an Information Memorandum to maintain confidentiality while providing key details about the business to potential buyers.

Confidentiality is critical to Arlind and his team in M&A transactions for several reasons. Firstly, disclosing sensitive information about the business, such as financial performance, strategic plans, or proprietary technology, to unauthorized parties can compromise the competitive position of the company and negatively impact its valuation. Moreover, leaks of confidential information can lead to reputational damage, loss of customer trust, and employee unrest, disrupting the business operations and undermining the success of the transaction.

Introduction to Non-Disclosure Agreements (NDAs) serves as a crucial step in safeguarding confidentiality in M&A transactions. NDAs are legally binding contracts that establish protections and obligations regarding the use and disclosure of confidential information shared between parties during the M&A process. By requiring potential buyers, advisors, and other stakeholders to sign NDAs before accessing confidential information, sellers can mitigate the risk of unauthorized disclosures and protect their proprietary assets.

NDAs typically include provisions outlining the scope of confidential information, restrictions on its use and disclosure, obligations to maintain confidentiality, and remedies for breaches of the agreement. These provisions ensure that parties understand their responsibilities and obligations regarding the protection of confidential information and provide recourse in the event of non-compliance or breaches of confidentiality.

Additionally, preparing an Confidential Information Memorandum (CIM) is essential for maintaining confidentiality while providing potential buyers with key details about the business. A CIM is a comprehensive document that provides an overview of the business, including its history, operations, financial performance, market position, and growth prospects. While an IM is designed to provide buyers with relevant information to evaluate the opportunity, it is essential to balance transparency with discretion to protect sensitive information.

The CIM should be carefully crafted to disclose pertinent details about the business while omitting proprietary or sensitive information that could compromise confidentiality. Sellers should work closely with their advisors to ensure that the IM strikes the right balance between transparency and confidentiality, highlighting the value proposition of the business without revealing sensitive information that could harm the competitive position or disrupt the transaction process. Maintaining confidentiality is paramount in M&A transactions to protect sensitive information and prevent disruptions to the business. Introduction to Non-Disclosure Agreements (NDAs) serves as a crucial step in safeguarding confidentiality by establishing legal protections and obligations regarding the use and disclosure of confidential information. Additionally, preparing an Information Memorandum provides potential buyers with key details about the business while maintaining confidentiality and discretion. By prioritizing confidentiality and implementing robust safeguards, sellers can navigate the complexities of Arlinds M&A transactions with confidence, knowing that their sensitive information is protected and secure. Screening buyers, employees, non-U.S. citizen buyers, and investors is a critical aspect of the mergers and acquisitions (M&A) process, essential for ensuring compatibility, mitigating risks, and safeguarding the interests of the seller. These screening processes involve evaluating qualifications, financial capabilities, and intentions to determine suitability and alignment with the seller's objectives. By conducting thorough due diligence and implementing screening protocols, sellers can identify qualified buyers and minimize the risk of encountering issues during the transaction process. First and foremost, screening buyers is essential to ensure that they possess the necessary qualifications, resources, and intentions to successfully complete the transaction. Sellers must evaluate the buyer's financial capabilities, industry experience, track record, and strategic objectives to determine their suitability as potential acquirers. By conducting thorough due diligence on buyers, sellers can assess their ability to finance the transaction, execute the deal, and preserve the value of the business post-acquisition. Screening employees involved in the transaction is crucial for maintaining continuity and stability within the organization. Sellers must assess the qualifications, integrity, and compatibility of key employees who will play a role in the transition process. By evaluating employees' skills, cultural fit, and commitment to the business, sellers can mitigate the risk of disruptions and ensure a smooth transition for both employees and the organization as a whole. Moreover, screening non-U.S. citizen buyers is essential to comply with regulatory requirements and safeguard national security interests. Sellers must assess the background, reputation, and intentions of non-U.S. citizen buyers to ensure that they do not pose any security risks or compliance concerns. By conducting thorough due diligence on non-U.S. citizen buyers, sellers can mitigate the risk of regulatory violations, reputational damage, and legal liabilities associated with foreign investment. Screening investors is essential for safeguarding the interests of the seller and preserving the integrity of the transaction process. Sellers must assess the financial stability, reputation, and alignment of investors with the seller's objectives and values. By evaluating investors' track record, investment philosophy, and risk appetite, sellers can ensure that they are partnering with reputable and reliable investors who can add value and support the growth and success of the business. Screening buyers, employees, non-U.S. citizen buyers, and investors is essential for ensuring compatibility, mitigating risks, and safeguarding the interests of the seller in M&A transactions. By conducting thorough due diligence and implementing screening protocols, sellers can identify qualified stakeholders who align with their objectives and values, minimize the risk of encountering issues during the transaction process, and maximize the likelihood of achieving successful outcomes. In the intricate landscape of mergers and acquisitions (M&A), avoiding tire kickers – individuals who express interest in a transaction without serious intent or financial capacity – is critical for preserving resources and maintaining focus on qualified prospects. Tire kickers can drain valuable time, energy, and resources from sellers, leading to delays, distractions, and missed opportunities. Therefore, implementing strategies to identify and deter tire kickers is essential for optimizing the M&A process and maximizing the likelihood of successful outcomes. One effective strategy for avoiding tire kickers is to implement pre-screening criteria to assess the qualifications and intentions of potential buyers or investors. Sellers can establish specific criteria, such as industry experience, financial stability, track record, and strategic fit, to evaluate the suitability of prospective stakeholders. By conducting preliminary due diligence and screening, sellers can identify qualified prospects who are genuinely interested and capable of pursuing the transaction, while filtering out individuals who lack the necessary qualifications or commitment. Moreover, requiring proof of financial capability is another effective way to deter tire kickers and ensure that potential buyers or investors have the resources to complete the transaction. Sellers can request financial statements, bank statements, or letters of credit to verify the financial capacity of prospective stakeholders and assess their ability to finance the deal. By setting clear expectations regarding the financial requirements of the transaction, sellers can deter individuals who lack the necessary resources or liquidity from engaging in the process, thereby minimizing the risk of encountering tire kickers. Furthermore, setting clear expectations regarding the transaction process and timeline is essential for managing the engagement of potential buyers or investors and avoiding tire kickers. Sellers can establish transparent communication channels, outline the steps involved in the M&A process, and establish deadlines and milestones to keep the transaction on track. By providing clear guidance and expectations upfront, sellers can deter tire kickers who are unwilling or unable to commit to the process, while attracting serious and qualified prospects who are prepared to move forward with the transaction. Avoiding tire kickers is critical for preserving resources and maintaining focus on qualified prospects in M&A transactions. By implementing pre-screening criteria, requiring proof of financial capability, and setting clear expectations regarding the transaction process and timeline, sellers can minimize the risk of encountering tire kickers and optimize the efficiency and effectiveness of the M&A process. By prioritizing engagement with qualified prospects who are genuinely interested and capable of completing the transaction, sellers can increase the likelihood of achieving successful outcomes and maximizing value creation in the dynamic landscape of mergers and acquisitions In the realm of mergers and acquisitions (M&A), having a seasoned advisor like Adam can significantly aid in avoiding tire kickers and streamlining the transaction process. Arlind's expertise and experience allow him to implement effective strategies and protocols to identify serious and qualified prospects while deterring individuals who lack genuine intent or financial capacity. One way Arlind helps in avoiding tire kickers is by leveraging his extensive network and industry connections to pre-screen potential buyers or investors. Through his vast network, Arlind can identify reputable and reliable stakeholders who have a track record of successful transactions and possess the financial resources to complete the deal. By tapping into his network, Arlind can filter out tire kickers and focus on engaging with qualified prospects who are serious about pursuing the transaction.

Arlind can assist sellers in setting clear expectations and requirements for potential buyers or investors, including proof of financial capability. By leveraging his expertise in deal structuring and negotiation, Arlind can help sellers establish transparent criteria for evaluating prospective stakeholders and ensure that only qualified individuals are allowed to proceed with the transaction. This proactive approach not only deters tire kickers but also streamlines the due diligence process and minimizes the risk of encountering issues during the transaction. Arlind's guidance and support throughout the transaction process enable sellers to navigate potential pitfalls and challenges effectively. From conducting thorough due diligence to negotiating terms and managing the closing process, Arlind ensures that sellers are well-equipped to make informed decisions and protect their interests throughout the deal lifecycle. By providing strategic advice and practical solutions, Arlind empowers sellers to focus their resources and attention on qualified prospects, maximizing the likelihood of achieving successful outcomes in the M&A transaction. Arlind's expertise, network, and guidance play a crucial role in avoiding tire kickers and optimizing the efficiency and effectiveness of the M&A process. By leveraging his industry knowledge, connections, and experience, Arlind helps sellers identify serious and qualified prospects, establish clear expectations, and navigate the complexities of the transaction with confidence and clarity. With Arlind's support, sellers can streamline the deal-making process, minimize risks, and maximize value creation in the dynamic landscape of mergers and acquisitions.

Effective marketing strategies are essential for identifying and engaging potential buyers or investors in the M&A market. By leveraging fishing and hunting approaches, utilizing ad portals, targeted campaigns, and other methods for finding buyers, sellers can increase visibility, generate interest, and maximize the likelihood of finding the right match for their business. Additionally, maintaining confidentiality, screening stakeholders, and avoiding tire kickers are crucial aspects of the M&A process that contribute to successful outcomes and mitigate risks for sellers.

Chapter 7: Meetings of the Minds

In the world of mergers and acquisitions (M&A), Chapter 7 explores the crucial phase of "Meetings of the Minds," where buyers and sellers come together to negotiate terms, align expectations, and ultimately reach agreements that shape the outcome of the transaction. This chapter delves into meeting the buyer, providing a guide to negotiating tactics, and unveiling the secret negotiating weapon that can tip the scales in favor of either party.

Meeting the buyer stands as a pivotal juncture in the intricate dance of mergers and acquisitions (M&A). It represents a crucial moment where sellers step onto the stage, face-to-face with potential acquirers, to embark on a journey of negotiation and collaboration. This encounter serves as a cornerstone of the M&A process, offering sellers the invaluable opportunity to directly engage with prospective buyers, establish rapport, and set the stage for fruitful negotiations.

Whether conducted in the hushed confines of a boardroom or the digital realms of virtual meetings, these encounters serve as more than just formalities; they are vibrant forums where ideas are exchanged, objectives are clarified, and visions are aligned. Sellers seize this moment to paint a vivid picture of their business, showcasing its strengths, potential, and value proposition. In turn, buyers scrutinize and evaluate, probing for insights, seeking synergies, and envisioning the possibilities that lie ahead. Central to these meetings is the exchange of information – a delicate dance where sellers unveil the inner workings of their business, sharing insights, financial data, and strategic plans with potential acquirers. Transparency reigns supreme as sellers strive to build trust and confidence with buyers, laying bare the foundations upon which successful negotiations are built. Through open communication and forthright dialogue, sellers foster an environment of mutual understanding and collaboration, paving the way for productive negotiations and deal-making. Moreover, these meetings provide sellers with a unique opportunity to explore potential synergies and value drivers with buyers. Sellers delve into the intricacies of their business model, highlighting areas of opportunity and potential growth. Buyers, in turn, bring their expertise and insights to the table, offering fresh perspectives and innovative ideas for unlocking value and driving growth post-acquisition. Through this exchange, sellers and buyers lay the groundwork for a partnership rooted in shared objectives and aligned interests. Whether face-to-face or mediated by screens and pixels, the essence of these meetings remains unchanged – to forge connections, foster understanding, and pave the way for successful negotiations and deal-making. Sellers seize this moment to make a lasting impression, showcasing the strengths and potential of their business while building trust and confidence with potential acquirers. In doing so, they set the stage for a journey of collaboration and partnership that has the potential to reshape industries, unlock value, and drive growth in the dynamic world of mergers and acquisitions. Negotiating tactics serve as the bedrock upon which the success of mergers and acquisitions (M&A) transactions is built. In the high-stakes arena of deal-making, the ability to navigate negotiations effectively can spell the difference between a favorable outcome and missed opportunities. This book delves into the critical role that negotiating tactics play in shaping the outcome of M&A transactions, providing insights into essential strategies and techniques for navigating the negotiation process effectively. Additionally, it highlights how M&A Adviser Arlind Sadiku, who mastered these tactics, can significantly influence the negotiation dynamics and drive successful outcomes. At the heart of negotiating tactics lies the art of influence, as parties seek to shape the terms, conditions, and overall value of the deal in their favor. Successful negotiators recognize that negotiation is not merely a zero-sum game but rather a collaborative process aimed at achieving mutual benefits while safeguarding individual interests. To this end, setting clear objectives and priorities is paramount, providing a roadmap for navigating negotiations and ensuring alignment with strategic goals. Understanding the other party's interests and motivations is equally crucial, as it enables negotiators to identify areas of common ground, anticipate potential points of contention, and craft solutions that address the underlying needs of both parties. By adopting a collaborative and empathetic approach, negotiators can foster trust and rapport, laying the foundation for constructive dialogue and creative problem-solving. Moreover, successful negotiators employ a range of tactics and techniques to achieve their desired outcomes while maintaining a collaborative and constructive dialogue. These tactics may include anchoring, framing, mirroring, and concession management, among others. Anchoring involves setting the tone of the negotiation by proposing an initial offer or position, while framing involves shaping the context of the discussion to influence perceptions and outcomes. Mirroring entails mirroring the behavior and communication style of the other party to establish rapport and build trust, while concession management involves strategically conceding on certain points to gain concessions in return. M&A Advisers like Arlind exemplify mastery in negotiating tactics, leveraging their expertise, experience, and intuition to navigate negotiations effectively and drive successful outcomes for their clients. Arlind's strategic approach to negotiation, coupled with his deep understanding of human psychology and behavior, enables him to anticipate and respond to the dynamics of the negotiation process with finesse and agility. Whether it's identifying areas of leverage, framing the discussion to favor his client's position, or managing concessions strategically, Arlind employs a range of tactics to achieve his client's objectives while maintaining a collaborative and constructive dialogue with the other party. Negotiating tactics play a critical role in shaping the outcome of M&A transactions, influencing the terms, conditions, and overall value of the deal. Successful negotiators recognize the importance of setting clear objectives, understanding the other party's interests and motivations, and employing a range of tactics and techniques to achieve their desired outcomes. Advisers like Arlind, who master these tactics, can significantly influence the negotiation dynamics and drive successful outcomes for their clients in the dynamic and competitive landscape of mergers and acquisitions. This unveils the secret negotiating weapon that can tip the scales in favor of either party: leverage. Leverage refers to the ability of one party to exert influence or control over the other party, often through a combination of strengths, weaknesses, and strategic positioning. Whether it's a unique asset, a strong market position, or alternative options, leverage can be a powerful tool in negotiations, enabling parties to secure favorable terms and outcomes that align with their objectives.

By meeting the buyer, understanding negotiating tactics, and leveraging their strengths effectively, sellers can navigate negotiations with confidence and achieve successful outcomes in the dynamic and competitive landscape of mergers and acquisitions.

Chapter 8: The Offer

In Chapter 8, "The Offer," we delve into the intricate process of negotiating and finalizing the terms of a merger or acquisition beyond just the price. This chapter explores how deal structure, conflicting objectives, and various factors shape the scope of negotiations. It also discusses negotiating the letter of intent, securing the offer with a deposit, timing considerations for taking the business off the market, considering earnouts, managing debt, escrow holdbacks, legal transaction structures (asset vs. stock sale), and the significance of non-compete agreements.

Negotiating the deal structure in a business acquisition is a multifaceted process that extends far beyond simply agreeing on a purchase price. While the price tag is undoubtedly a critical aspect of the deal, crafting the terms and structure of the transaction is equally, if not more, important. This intricate process involves finding common ground between the buyer and seller to create a framework that satisfies the interests and objectives of both parties.

At the heart of negotiating the deal structure is the need to address various financial and operational considerations. These include determining payment schedules, allocating risks and liabilities, defining the scope of assets or shares being acquired, and establishing any post-closing arrangements. Each of these elements plays a crucial role in shaping the overall structure of the deal and can have significant implications for both parties involved.

One of the key challenges in negotiating the deal structure is managing conflicting objectives between buyers and sellers. Naturally, each party enters the negotiation process with its own set of priorities, preferences, and concerns. Buyers typically aim to minimize upfront costs, maximize control over the acquired assets or business, and mitigate risks associated with the transaction. On the other hand, sellers seek to maximize the value they receive for their business, minimize tax liabilities, and protect themselves from potential liabilities post-sale.

Navigating these conflicting objectives requires a delicate balance of compromise, creativity, and effective communication. Both parties must be willing to make concessions and explore alternative solutions to address each other's concerns while safeguarding their own interests. This often involves trade-offs where one party may agree to certain terms in exchange for concessions on other aspects of the deal.

Effective communication is essential throughout the negotiation process to ensure that both parties understand each other's perspectives and concerns. Clear and transparent communication fosters trust and helps build rapport between the buyer and seller, making it easier to find common ground and reach mutually acceptable agreements.

In addition to addressing financial and operational considerations, negotiating the deal structure also involves navigating legal and regulatory requirements. This may include conducting due diligence, drafting and negotiating legal agreements such as purchase agreements and ancillary documents, and obtaining any necessary approvals or consents from regulatory authorities or third parties.

Ultimately, the goal of negotiating the deal structure is to create a win-win scenario where both parties can achieve their objectives and walk away from the transaction satisfied. By approaching the negotiation process with a spirit of collaboration, flexibility, and creativity, buyers and sellers can overcome challenges, find common ground, and create value through the acquisition.

Negotiating the scope of a business transaction involves navigating a myriad of factors that can influence the terms, conditions, and overall structure of the deal. These factors range from the complexity of the transaction itself to regulatory requirements, prevailing market conditions, and the strategic significance of the deal to both parties involved. Among the crucial steps in this negotiation process is crafting the letter of intent (LOI), a document that serves as a preliminary agreement outlining the key terms and conditions of the offer.

The complexity of the transaction plays a significant role in shaping the scope of negotiations. More complex deals, such as those involving multiple parties, intricate legal structures, or significant regulatory hurdles, often require more extensive negotiations to address various complexities and contingencies. Conversely, simpler transactions may involve fewer negotiation points but still require careful consideration to ensure that all essential aspects of the deal are adequately addressed.

Regulatory considerations also play a crucial role in determining the scope of negotiations. Different industries and jurisdictions may have specific regulations and compliance requirements that need to be addressed as part of the transaction. Negotiating the terms of the deal in light of these regulations ensures that both parties remain compliant and avoid any potential legal pitfalls or regulatory challenges down the line.

Market conditions can also influence the scope of negotiations, particularly regarding pricing, valuation, and financing terms. In a competitive market, where demand for acquisition targets is high, negotiations may be more challenging as buyers and sellers vie for favorable terms. Conversely, in a buyer's market, where supply outweighs demand, sellers may need to be more flexible in their negotiation approach to attract potential buyers.

The strategic importance of the deal to both parties is another critical factor that influences the scope of negotiations. Deals that are deemed strategically significant, such as acquisitions that offer access to new markets, technologies, or capabilities, may involve more extensive negotiations to ensure that both parties' strategic objectives are met. Negotiating the terms of the deal in alignment with these strategic objectives is essential for driving value and achieving long-term success.

At the heart of negotiating the scope of the transaction is the process of formalizing the terms of the offer through the letter of intent (LOI). The LOI serves as a roadmap for the transaction, outlining key terms such as purchase price, payment terms, due diligence requirements, and any contingencies or conditions precedent to closing. Negotiating the LOI allows both parties to clarify their expectations, identify any potential areas of disagreement, and lay the groundwork for further negotiations.

Securing the offer with a deposit is another critical step in the negotiation process, providing assurance to both parties and demonstrating commitment to moving forward with the transaction. The deposit serves as a tangible sign of good faith, indicating the buyer's seriousness and willingness to proceed with the deal. For sellers, the deposit provides a level of security and compensation for taking the property off the market while negotiations continue.

Negotiating the scope of a business transaction involves navigating a complex interplay of factors, including transaction complexity, regulatory requirements, market conditions, and strategic considerations. Crafting the letter of intent and securing the offer with a deposit are critical steps in this process, setting the stage for further negotiations and ultimately facilitating a successful outcome for both parties involved.

Timing considerations are paramount in the process of selling a business, particularly when it comes to deciding the opportune moment to take the business off the market. This decision involves striking a delicate balance between the imperative of maintaining confidentiality and discretion and the desire to maximize options and opportunities for the sale. Additionally, the incorporation of earnouts into the deal structure offers a flexible payment mechanism that allows sellers to receive additional compensation contingent upon the future performance of the business. Earnouts serve to align incentives between buyers and sellers, mitigate risks, and enhance the overall appeal of the deal.

Maintaining confidentiality and discretion is crucial during the initial stages of the sale process. Sellers typically prefer to keep their intention to sell confidential to avoid any potential negative consequences, such as employee uncertainty, customer defections, or competitor interference. However, keeping a business on the market indefinitely can lead to diminishing returns and may signal to potential buyers that the business is undesirable or overpriced. Therefore, sellers must carefully assess market conditions, gauge buyer interest, and determine the optimal timing to take the business off the market.

Taking the business off the market at the right time is essential to maximizing options and opportunities for the sale. By limiting the availability of the business to a select group of serious buyers, sellers can create a sense of urgency and competition, driving up the perceived value of the business and increasing the likelihood of securing favorable terms. However, sellers must strike a balance between maximizing options and rushing the process, as overly aggressive tactics can deter potential buyers and undermine the credibility of the sale.

Earnouts offer sellers a flexible payment structure that can enhance the attractiveness of the deal and mitigate risks associated with uncertain future performance. Under an earnout arrangement, a portion of the purchase price is contingent upon the achievement of specified performance targets or milestones post-closing. This incentivizes sellers to remain actively involved in the business during the transition period and aligns their interests with those of the buyer in maximizing the business's future success.

From the buyer's perspective, earnouts provide a level of assurance that the seller's representations regarding the business's performance are accurate and realistic. By tying a portion of the purchase price to future performance, buyers can mitigate the risk of overpaying for a business that fails to meet expectations post-acquisition. Additionally, earnouts can facilitate smoother negotiations by allowing buyers and sellers to bridge valuation gaps and reach mutually acceptable terms.

In conclusion, timing considerations are critical in determining when to take a business off the market, balancing confidentiality and discretion with the need to maximize options and opportunities for the sale. Earnouts offer a flexible payment structure that aligns incentives between buyers and sellers, mitigates risks, and enhances the overall appeal of the deal. By carefully assessing market conditions, gauging buyer interest, and incorporating earnouts into the deal structure, sellers can optimize their chances of achieving a successful sale outcome.

Managing debt is a critical aspect of mergers and acquisitions (M&A) transactions, as it can have significant implications for both buyers and sellers. Buyers, in particular, must carefully evaluate the impact of assuming or refinancing existing debt obligations as part of the transaction. Additionally, escrow holdbacks serve as a vital mechanism for securing funds to address potential post-closing liabilities or contingencies, thereby ensuring that both parties fulfill their obligations under the agreement.

When considering an M&A transaction, buyers must assess the target company's existing debt obligations and evaluate how assuming or refinancing these obligations will affect the overall financial structure of the deal. Assuming existing debt can provide buyers with access to favorable financing terms and may be advantageous if the debt is at a lower interest rate or has favorable repayment terms. However, assuming significant debt obligations can also increase the buyer's leverage and financial risk, particularly if the target company's financial performance deteriorates post-acquisition.

On the other hand, refinancing existing debt allows buyers to replace the target company's debt with new financing that better aligns with their strategic objectives and risk tolerance. Refinancing can help buyers secure more favorable terms, extend repayment periods, or consolidate debt into a single loan, thereby improving cash flow and financial flexibility. However, refinancing may also involve transaction costs and may be subject to lender approval, adding complexity to the deal process.

Escrow holdbacks play a crucial role in managing the risks associated with M&A transactions, particularly in addressing potential post-closing liabilities or contingencies. As part of the purchase agreement, a portion of the purchase price is placed in escrow and held by a neutral third party until certain conditions are met or resolved. This provides assurance to both parties that funds are available to address any unforeseen issues that arise after the closing, such as undisclosed liabilities, breaches of representations or warranties, or pending litigation.

Escrow holdbacks serve as a form of security for the buyer, ensuring that funds are available to cover any losses or damages resulting from the seller's failure to meet its obligations under the agreement. At the same time, escrow holdbacks provide protection for the seller by safeguarding a portion of the purchase price until all post-closing obligations have been fulfilled. By mitigating risks and uncertainties, escrow holdbacks help facilitate smoother transactions and foster trust and confidence between buyers and sellers.

Managing debt and addressing potential post-closing liabilities are critical considerations in M&A transactions. Buyers must carefully evaluate the impact of assuming or refinancing existing debt obligations, weighing the potential benefits against the associated risks. Escrow holdbacks provide a valuable mechanism for securing funds to address post-closing contingencies, ensuring that both parties fulfill their obligations and minimizing the likelihood of disputes or litigation arising after the transaction is completed. By effectively managing debt and utilizing escrow holdbacks, buyers and sellers can enhance the likelihood of a successful and mutually beneficial transaction.

The legal transaction structure is a critical aspect of mergers and acquisitions (M&A) that has far-reaching implications for both buyers and sellers. Two common transaction structures are asset sales and stock sales, each carrying its own set of advantages, disadvantages, and implications for tax treatment, liability exposure, and operational flexibility.

In an asset sale, the buyer purchases specific assets and liabilities of the target company, rather than acquiring the company itself. This approach allows the buyer to cherry-pick the assets they desire while leaving behind any unwanted liabilities or obligations. From a tax perspective, asset sales can offer potential tax benefits for both parties. Buyers may benefit from the ability to depreciate or amortize the acquired assets for tax purposes, while sellers may be able to offset any gains with losses from retained assets or liabilities. However, asset sales can also be more complex and time-consuming, requiring careful negotiation and documentation of asset transfers and liabilities assumptions.

On the other hand, a stock sale involves the purchase of the target company's shares or ownership interests. This approach results in the buyer acquiring the entire business entity, along with all of its assets, liabilities, contracts, and obligations. From a tax standpoint, stock sales can offer simplicity and efficiency, as they typically result in a single level of taxation at the shareholder level. However, buyers may assume all existing liabilities and obligations of the target company, including potential unknown or undisclosed liabilities. Additionally, stock sales may limit the buyer's ability to step up the tax basis of the acquired assets, potentially resulting in higher future tax liabilities.

Non-compete agreements are another essential component of M&A transactions, particularly in industries where competition is fierce and intellectual property is valuable. These agreements serve to protect the buyer's interests by restricting sellers from competing in the same market or industry after the transaction is completed. Non-compete agreements typically specify the duration, geographic scope, and prohibited activities, and may also include provisions for compensation or other consideration to the seller. By preventing sellers from engaging in competitive activities post-sale, non-compete agreements help safeguard the value of the acquired business and preserve the buyer's competitive advantage.

The legal transaction structure, whether it be an asset sale or a stock sale, has significant implications for tax treatment, liability exposure, and operational flexibility in M&A transactions. Buyers and sellers must carefully consider the pros and cons of each structure and negotiate terms that align with their respective objectives and interests. Additionally, non-compete agreements play a crucial role in protecting the buyer's interests and preserving the value of the acquired business by restricting sellers from engaging in competitive activities post-sale. By understanding and addressing these legal considerations, parties can mitigate risks, maximize value, and ensure the success of their M&A transactions.

The multifaceted nature of negotiating "The Offer" in M&A transactions, emphasizing the importance of considering factors beyond just the price. By focusing on deal structure, balancing conflicting objectives, and addressing key considerations such as timing, earnouts, debt management, and legal structure, parties can navigate negotiations effectively and achieve successful outcomes in the dynamic and complex landscape of mergers and acquisitions.

Chapter 9: The Due Diligence

Chapter 9, "The Due Diligence," explores the critical phase of investigating and evaluating the target company's affairs, operations, and financials before finalizing a merger or acquisition. This book delves into the purpose of due diligence, provides a sample due diligence checklist, discusses transferring the lease, allocating the purchase price for tax purposes, and considers how the entity structure affects deal structure.

Halfway There - The Purpose of Due Diligence:
In the world of mergers and acquisitions (M&A), due diligence stands as a crucial milestone, marking the halfway point in the journey towards completing a transaction. This pivotal process serves as a comprehensive examination of the target company's internal and external affairs, providing buyers with a deep dive into the intricacies of the business. Its primary purpose is to equip buyers with a thorough understanding of the risks, opportunities, and liabilities associated with the transaction, empowering them to make informed decisions and effectively mitigate risks.

At its core, due diligence encompasses a wide range of activities aimed at uncovering key insights and evaluating various aspects of the target company. Financial due diligence involves scrutinizing the target's financial statements, cash flow projections, and historical performance to assess its financial health and viability. Operational due diligence focuses on evaluating the target's operational capabilities, including its management team, supply chain, infrastructure, and technological systems. Legal due diligence involves reviewing contracts, licenses, permits, and regulatory filings to ensure compliance with applicable laws and regulations. Strategic due diligence assesses the alignment of the target company with the buyer's strategic objectives and market dynamics, identifying synergies, opportunities for growth, and potential integration challenges.

By conducting due diligence, buyers gain invaluable insights into the target company's strengths, weaknesses, opportunities, and threats, enabling them to make well-informed decisions throughout the transaction process. It allows buyers to identify potential deal breakers, such as undisclosed liabilities, regulatory issues, or material adverse changes, and negotiate appropriate protections or adjustments to the transaction terms. Additionally, due diligence helps buyers assess the target company's valuation, identify areas for value creation or enhancement, and develop post-acquisition integration plans to ensure a smooth transition and maximize the value of the transaction.

Furthermore, due diligence serves as a risk management tool, enabling buyers to identify and mitigate potential risks and uncertainties associated with the transaction. By uncovering any hidden or undisclosed issues early in the process, buyers can avoid costly surprises and ensure that the transaction proceeds smoothly. This proactive approach to risk management helps protect the buyer's interests and minimizes the likelihood of post-closing disputes or litigation.

Due diligence plays a critical role in the M&A process, serving as a comprehensive examination of the target company's internal and external affairs. By conducting due diligence, buyers can gain a thorough understanding of the risks, opportunities, and liabilities associated with the transaction, enabling informed decision-making and effective risk mitigation. As the halfway point in the M&A journey, due diligence empowers buyers to navigate the complexities of the transaction process with confidence and clarity, ultimately leading to successful outcomes for all parties involved.

Navigating the intricate landscape of mergers and acquisitions (M&A) requires a meticulous approach, with due diligence standing as a cornerstone of the process. A sample due diligence checklist serves as a roadmap, outlining the critical areas and documents that buyers must review to gain a comprehensive understanding of the target company. This checklist encompasses a broad spectrum of information, ranging from financial statements to regulatory filings, contracts, and intellectual property rights. As buyers embark on this journey, the expertise and guidance of an experienced M&A Advisor like Arlind can prove invaluable in navigating the complexities of the due diligence process and ensuring a successful transaction outcome.

The sample due diligence checklist serves as a structured framework for buyers to systematically evaluate the target company's affairs and uncover any potential risks, opportunities, or liabilities. Financial statements and tax returns provide insight into the target's financial health, performance trends, and tax obligations, enabling buyers to assess the company's profitability, liquidity, and solvency. Contracts and agreements offer visibility into the target's contractual relationships with customers, suppliers, employees, and other stakeholders, highlighting any obligations, restrictions, or contingencies that may impact the transaction.

Regulatory filings and compliance documents help buyers assess the target's legal and regulatory standing, ensuring compliance with applicable laws, regulations, and industry standards. Intellectual property rights, including patents, trademarks, copyrights, and trade secrets, represent valuable assets that require careful scrutiny to confirm ownership, validity, and enforceability. Employee records shed light on the target's workforce, including employment agreements, compensation plans, benefits, and potential liabilities related to employment disputes or litigation.

As buyers navigate the due diligence process, Arlind, as an M&A Advisor, can provide invaluable assistance and guidance at every step of the way. With his expertise and industry knowledge, Arlind can help buyers interpret and analyze the information gathered from the due diligence checklist, identifying key insights, trends, and areas of concern. Arlind's experience in negotiating and structuring M&A transactions allows him to anticipate potential issues and formulate strategies to address them effectively, minimizing risks and maximizing value for his clients.

Arlind can also leverage his network of industry contacts and resources to conduct targeted due diligence investigations, gathering additional information and insights to supplement the findings of the checklist. This proactive approach enables buyers to uncover any hidden or undisclosed issues early in the process, allowing them to address them proactively and negotiate appropriate protections in the purchase agreement.

Furthermore, Arlind can serve as a trusted advisor and advocate for buyers throughout the due diligence process, liaising with other professionals, such as legal counsel, accountants, and valuation experts, to ensure a comprehensive and thorough review of the target company's affairs. By leveraging Arlind's expertise and guidance, buyers can navigate the complexities of the due diligence process with confidence and clarity, ultimately leading to a successful transaction outcome.

A sample due diligence checklist serves as a critical tool for buyers to evaluate the target company's affairs and identify potential risks and opportunities. With the guidance and support of an experienced M&A Advisor like Arlind, buyers can navigate the due diligence process with confidence, leveraging his expertise, industry knowledge, and resources to uncover key insights, address potential issues, and negotiate favorable terms in the transaction agreement. By partnering with Arlind, buyers can ensure a smooth and successful M&A transaction that maximizes value and mitigates risks for all parties involved.

Transferring the Lease:
Transferring the lease represents a pivotal step in the due diligence process of a merger or acquisition, especially for businesses reliant on leased premises for their operations. It entails a comprehensive review of the lease agreement's terms and conditions, evaluation of any restrictions or obligations related to assignment or subleasing, and negotiation with the landlord to obtain approval for the transfer. Neglecting to address lease transfer matters adequately can result in operational disruptions and potential legal conflicts, underscoring the importance of careful attention to this aspect of due diligence.

For buyers, reviewing the terms and conditions of the lease agreement is paramount. This involves scrutinizing key provisions such as the lease term, rent amount, renewal options, maintenance responsibilities, and any special clauses or restrictions that may impact the transfer process. Understanding these terms is essential for assessing the financial implications and operational constraints associated with the lease and determining the feasibility of the transaction.

Assessing any restrictions or obligations related to assignment or subleasing is another critical aspect of lease transfer due diligence. Many lease agreements contain provisions that govern the transfer of the lease to a new owner or the subleasing of the premises to a third party. Buyers must carefully review these provisions to determine the landlord's requirements for approval and any conditions or limitations imposed on the transfer. Failure to comply with these requirements can result in the landlord withholding consent or imposing penalties, jeopardizing the viability of the transaction.

Negotiating with the landlord to secure approval for the lease transfer is often a complex and time-consuming process. Buyers must engage in proactive communication with the landlord, providing them with all necessary information and assurances to facilitate the transfer smoothly. This may involve demonstrating the buyer's financial stability, operational expertise, and commitment to fulfilling the terms of the lease. Additionally, buyers may need to address any concerns or objections raised by the landlord and negotiate favorable terms for the transfer, such as rent adjustments or lease modifications.

Failing to address lease transfer issues can have serious consequences for the buyer. Operational disruptions, loss of access to critical facilities, and potential legal disputes with the landlord are just a few of the risks associated with improperly executed lease transfers. Therefore, buyers must prioritize this aspect of due diligence and allocate sufficient time and resources to address any issues that may arise.

Transferring the lease is a critical aspect of due diligence in mergers and acquisitions, particularly for businesses operating from leased premises. Buyers must carefully review the terms and conditions of the lease agreement, assess any restrictions or obligations related to assignment or subleasing, and negotiate with the landlord to secure approval for the transfer. By addressing lease transfer matters diligently, buyers can mitigate risks and ensure a smooth transition of operations following the transaction.

Give the Tax Man His Cut - Allocating the Purchase Price:
In the realm of mergers and acquisitions (M&A), allocating the purchase price is not merely an administrative task but a strategic decision with significant implications for both buyers and sellers, particularly from a tax perspective. This process involves assigning the total purchase price of the transaction to specific assets or categories, thereby determining the tax consequences that will follow. Whether it's capital gains, 1031 exchanges, depreciation recapture, or tax basis adjustments, careful tax planning and allocation play a pivotal role in minimizing tax liabilities and maximizing tax benefits for both parties involved.

For sellers, the allocation of the purchase price has direct implications on the amount of taxable gain realized from the transaction. The tax treatment of gains derived from the sale of different types of assets, such as tangible assets, intangible assets, and goodwill, varies considerably. By strategically allocating the purchase price among these assets, sellers can optimize their tax position, potentially reducing their overall tax burden and maximizing after-tax proceeds from the transaction. Additionally, proper allocation can help sellers take advantage of preferential tax rates or capital gains exemptions available for certain types of assets.

On the other hand, buyers must also consider the tax implications of the purchase price allocation, particularly in terms of tax basis adjustments and future tax deductions. The allocation of the purchase price to specific assets establishes their tax basis for depreciation or amortization purposes, affecting the amount of future tax deductions that buyers can claim. By structuring the allocation strategically, buyers can enhance their tax efficiency and maximize the benefits of tax deductions over time, thereby improving the overall return on investment from the acquisition.

Furthermore, the allocation of the purchase price can also impact the feasibility of certain tax-deferred transactions, such as like-kind exchanges under Section 1031 of the Internal Revenue Code. By allocating a portion of the purchase price to qualifying assets eligible for exchange, buyers can potentially defer recognition of capital gains taxes, providing them with additional liquidity and flexibility to reinvest in other opportunities.

Allocating the purchase price is a critical consideration for both buyers and sellers in M&A transactions, with significant implications for tax planning and optimization. By strategically allocating the purchase price among different assets or categories, parties can minimize tax liabilities, maximize tax benefits, and enhance the overall financial outcomes of the transaction. With careful tax planning and allocation, both buyers and sellers can ensure that they "give the tax man his cut" in the most efficient and advantageous manner possible, maximizing value and mitigating risks for all parties involved.

In the intricate landscape of mergers and acquisitions (M&A), the entity structure of the target company plays a pivotal role in shaping the deal structure and terms of the transaction. Whether the transaction takes the form of an asset purchase or stock purchase depends on a multitude of factors, including liability exposure, tax treatment, and operational considerations. Buyers must meticulously assess the implications of the target company's entity structure on the deal structure and negotiate accordingly to achieve their strategic objectives.

The decision between an asset purchase and a stock purchase hinges on the legal and financial attributes of the target company's entity structure. In an asset purchase, the buyer acquires specific assets and liabilities of the target company, allowing them to cherry-pick desirable assets while leaving behind unwanted liabilities. This structure provides buyers with greater control over which assets they acquire and can mitigate risks associated with unknown or undisclosed liabilities. Additionally, asset purchases may offer tax advantages, as buyers can depreciate or amortize the acquired assets for tax purposes, potentially reducing their overall tax liabilities.

On the other hand, a stock purchase involves acquiring the target company's shares or ownership interests, effectively transferring ownership of the entire entity, along with all assets, liabilities, contracts, and obligations. While stock purchases offer simplicity and efficiency, as they typically result in a single level of taxation at the shareholder level,

they also entail assuming all existing liabilities and obligations of the target company. Buyers must carefully evaluate the potential risks and liabilities associated with stock purchases and conduct thorough due diligence to assess the target's financial and legal standing.
The entity structure of the target company also influences other aspects of the deal structure, such as financing arrangements, post-closing integration, and employee retention. For example, in an asset purchase, buyers may have greater flexibility in structuring financing arrangements, as lenders may be more willing to finance specific assets rather than the entire entity. Additionally, buyers may need to negotiate new contracts or agreements with suppliers, customers, and employees following an asset purchase, whereas these relationships may remain unchanged in a stock purchase. Moreover, the entity structure of the target company can have implications for tax planning and optimization strategies. Buyers must consider the tax consequences of both asset and stock purchases, including potential capital gains, depreciation recapture, and tax basis adjustments. By understanding the tax implications associated with each structure, buyers can make informed decisions and implement tax-efficient strategies to minimize tax liabilities and maximize after-tax proceeds from the transaction. The entity structure of the target company plays a critical role in determining the deal structure and terms of an M&A transaction. Whether the transaction takes the form of an asset purchase or stock purchase depends on various factors, including liability exposure, tax treatment, and operational considerations. Buyers must carefully evaluate these factors and negotiate accordingly to achieve their strategic objectives and maximize value from the transaction. By understanding how the entity structure affects deal structure, buyers can navigate the complexities of M&A transactions with confidence and clarity, ultimately leading to successful outcomes for all parties involved. The importance of due diligence in M&A transactions, providing buyers with valuable insights and information to make informed decisions and mitigate risks effectively. By conducting a thorough due diligence process, addressing key considerations such as lease transfer, tax allocation, and entity structure, buyers can navigate the complexities of M&A transactions with confidence and achieve successful outcomes in the dynamic and competitive landscape of mergers and acquisitions.

Chapter 10: The Closing

Chapter 10, "The Closing," marks the culmination of the merger or acquisition process, where all parties come together to finalize the transaction and transfer ownership of the target company. This chapter provides an overview of the closing process, preparing for the closing, negotiating the purchase agreement, representations and warranties, indemnification, escrow, closing day, and post-closing considerations.

The Final Days - Overview of the Closing Process:
As the culmination of months of meticulous planning and negotiation, the closing process represents the final stage in the journey of a merger or acquisition (M&A) transaction. This pivotal phase involves coordinating various aspects of the deal, including legal documentation, financial arrangements, and regulatory compliance, to ensure a smooth and seamless transition of ownership. During this critical period, parties finalize the terms of the purchase agreement, prepare closing documents, and address any outstanding issues or contingencies before completing the transaction.

At the outset of the closing process, parties typically review and finalize the terms of the purchase agreement, ensuring that all parties are in alignment with the agreed-upon terms and conditions of the transaction. This may involve resolving any last-minute negotiations or adjustments to the deal structure, addressing contingencies, and obtaining necessary approvals or consents from stakeholders or regulatory authorities.

Once the terms of the purchase agreement are finalized, parties begin the process of preparing closing documents, which may include legal agreements, transfer documents, financing arrangements, and other necessary paperwork. These documents serve to formalize the transaction and transfer ownership of the target company from the seller to the buyer. Legal counsel plays a crucial role in drafting and reviewing these documents, ensuring that they accurately reflect the terms of the agreement and comply with applicable laws and regulations.

In addition to preparing closing documents, parties must also address any outstanding issues or contingencies that may arise during the final days leading up to the closing date. This may include resolving disputes, obtaining necessary approvals or clearances, satisfying closing conditions, and coordinating with third-party service providers, such as lenders, insurers, or regulatory agencies.

Throughout the closing process, Arlind, as an experienced M&A Adviser, can provide invaluable assistance and guidance to both buyers and sellers. With his expertise and industry knowledge, Arlind can help parties navigate the complexities of the closing process, anticipate potential issues or challenges, and ensure that all necessary steps are taken to facilitate a successful transaction.

Arlind can assist parties in reviewing and finalizing the terms of the purchase agreement, negotiating any last-minute adjustments or concessions, and coordinating with legal counsel to ensure that closing documents are prepared accurately and in a timely manner. He can also help parties identify and address any outstanding issues or contingencies, leveraging his network of industry contacts and resources to resolve issues efficiently and minimize delays.

Arlind can serve as a trusted advisor and advocate for parties throughout the closing process, providing reassurance, guidance, and support as they navigate the final stages of the transaction. By partnering with Arlind, parties can navigate the complexities of the closing process with confidence and clarity, ensuring a smooth and successful transition of ownership for all parties involved.

The closing process represents the culmination of an M&A transaction, where parties finalize the terms of the purchase agreement, prepare closing documents, and address any outstanding issues or contingencies before completing the transaction. With the assistance of an experienced M&A Adviser like Arlind, parties can navigate the complexities of the closing process with confidence, ensuring a smooth and successful transition of ownership and maximizing value from the transaction.

Almost There - Preparing for the Closing:

As the closing date of a merger or acquisition (M&A) transaction draws near, parties must focus their efforts on ensuring that all necessary preparations are made to facilitate a seamless and successful transition of ownership. Preparing for the closing involves a comprehensive review of all aspects of the transaction, including legal documentation, regulatory compliance, financial arrangements, and due diligence matters. This critical phase requires careful coordination and attention to detail to mitigate risks and uncertainties and ensure a smooth execution of the transaction.

One of the key tasks in preparing for the closing is ensuring that all necessary documents, approvals, and conditions precedent are in place. This may involve finalizing and executing legal agreements, transfer documents, financing arrangements, and other closing documents required to formalize the transaction. Legal counsel plays a crucial role in overseeing this process, ensuring that all documents are accurately prepared, reviewed, and executed in accordance with applicable laws and regulations.

Additionally, parties must obtain any required regulatory approvals or clearances to proceed with the transaction. This may include antitrust approvals, industry-specific regulations, or approvals from government agencies or regulatory bodies. Securing these approvals is essential to ensuring the legality and validity of the transaction and avoiding potential delays or complications during the closing process.

Another important aspect of preparing for the closing is addressing any outstanding disputes or issues that may arise during the final stages of the transaction. This may involve resolving disagreements between parties, negotiating settlements, or obtaining waivers or consents from third parties. By addressing these issues proactively, parties can minimize the risk of last-minute obstacles derailing the closing process.

All parties must finalize any remaining due diligence matters to ensure that all material information has been reviewed and addressed before closing. This may involve conducting final reviews of financial statements, legal documents, operational records, and other relevant information to confirm the accuracy and completeness of the information provided. By conducting thorough due diligence, parties can identify and mitigate any remaining risks or uncertainties that may impact the transaction.

Throughout the preparation process, Arlind, as an experienced M&A Adviser, can provide invaluable assistance and guidance to parties involved in the transaction. With his expertise and industry knowledge, Adam can help parties navigate the complexities of preparing for the closing, anticipate potential issues or challenges, and ensure that all necessary steps are taken to facilitate a smooth and successful transaction.

Arlind can assist parties in coordinating with legal counsel to finalize and execute closing documents, obtaining regulatory approvals, and resolving any outstanding disputes or issues that may arise. He can also help parties conduct final due diligence reviews to ensure that all material information has been thoroughly reviewed and addressed before closing. By leveraging his global network of industry contacts and resources, Arlind can expedite the preparation process and minimize delays, ensuring that parties are fully prepared for a successful closing.

Preparing for the closing of an M&A transaction requires careful coordination and attention to detail to ensure a smooth and successful transition of ownership. By focusing on finalizing documents, obtaining regulatory approvals, resolving disputes, and completing due diligence matters, parties can mitigate risks and uncertainties and maximize the likelihood of a successful closing. With the assistance of an experienced M&A Adviser like Arlind, all parties can navigate the complexities of preparing for the closing with confidence and clarity, ensuring a seamless transition and maximizing value from the transaction.
paring for the closing entails ensuring that all necessary documents, approvals, and conditions precedent are in place to facilitate the smooth execution of the transaction. This may include obtaining regulatory approvals, securing financing, resolving outstanding disputes, and finalizing any remaining due diligence matters to mitigate risks and uncertainties.

Negotiating the Purchase Agreement:
In the complex landscape of mergers and acquisitions (M&A), negotiating the purchase agreement stands as a pivotal step in the closing process. This phase involves finalizing the terms and conditions of the transaction, ranging from the purchase price and payment terms to representations and warranties, indemnification provisions, and closing conditions. Effective negotiation during this stage requires parties to balance their interests, identify common ground, and address potential areas of disagreement to reach a mutually acceptable agreement that facilitates a smooth and successful transaction.

At the heart of negotiating the purchase agreement lies the determination of the purchase price, which serves as a cornerstone of the transaction. Buyers and sellers must engage in thorough discussions and analysis to arrive at a price that accurately reflects the value of the target company and aligns with their respective objectives. This may involve considering various valuation methods, market trends, financial projections, and synergies to determine a fair and equitable price that satisfies both parties.

In addition to the purchase price, parties must negotiate the payment terms of the transaction, including the structure of consideration (e.g., cash, stock, or a combination thereof) and any earn-out or contingent payment arrangements. These terms play a crucial role in determining the financial implications of the transaction and may impact the overall value and risk allocation between the parties. Negotiating payment terms requires careful consideration of liquidity, tax implications, financing arrangements, and future performance expectations.

Representations and warranties are another key component of the purchase agreement, providing assurances to the buyer regarding the accuracy and completeness of information disclosed by the seller. Negotiating these provisions involves identifying the scope and breadth of representations and warranties, allocating risk between the parties, and determining any limitations or exclusions to liability. Sellers seek to limit their exposure by qualifying or narrowing the scope of representations and warranties, while buyers aim to obtain comprehensive assurances to protect their interests.

Indemnification provisions also play a critical role in negotiating the purchase agreement, outlining the parties' respective obligations in the event of breaches of representations, warranties, or covenants. Negotiating these provisions involves determining the scope of indemnification, limitations on liability, and procedures for resolving disputes. Buyers seek robust indemnification provisions to protect against potential losses or liabilities, while sellers aim to limit their exposure and preserve their assets.

Furthermore, negotiating closing conditions is essential to ensuring that the transaction proceeds smoothly and efficiently. These conditions may include obtaining regulatory approvals, securing financing, satisfying due diligence requirements, and fulfilling any other obligations specified in the agreement. Negotiating closing conditions involves balancing the need for certainty and flexibility, identifying potential obstacles or contingencies, and establishing clear timelines and milestones for closing.

Arlind, as an experienced M&A Adviser with a global network, can provide invaluable assistance and guidance to parties involved in negotiating the purchase agreement. With his expertise and industry knowledge, Arlind can help parties navigate the complexities of the negotiation process, identify areas of opportunity or risk, and develop strategies to achieve their objectives effectively. Arlind's global network enables him to provide insights into market trends, regulatory requirements, and cultural nuances that may impact the negotiation process, allowing parties to make informed decisions and reach mutually beneficial agreements.

Negotiating the purchase agreement is a critical aspect of the closing process in mergers and acquisitions. Effective negotiation requires parties to balance their interests, identify common ground, and address potential areas of disagreement to reach a mutually acceptable agreement that facilitates a smooth and successful transaction. With the assistance of an experienced M&A Adviser like Arlind, parties can navigate the complexities of the negotiation process with confidence and clarity, ensuring that their interests are protected and their objectives are achieved.

Not So Fast - Representations and Warranties:
In the intricate world of mergers and acquisitions (M&A), representations and warranties stand as critical components of the purchase agreement, serving to safeguard the interests of both buyers and sellers. These statements, made by the seller, provide assurances regarding the condition, performance, and legality of the target company's business and assets. Representations and warranties play a crucial role in mitigating risks and uncertainties for the buyer by offering assurances about the accuracy and completeness of information disclosed during due diligence and negotiations.

At the heart of representations and warranties lies the principle of transparency and disclosure. Sellers are obligated to provide buyers with accurate and comprehensive information about the target company, its operations, financial condition, assets, liabilities, contracts, and legal compliance. These assurances serve to instill confidence in the buyer and provide a basis for evaluating the risks and opportunities associated with the transaction.

Representations typically cover a wide range of areas, including financial statements, operational matters, intellectual property rights, employee matters, compliance with laws and regulations, environmental issues, and litigation matters, among others. Each representation is carefully crafted to address specific aspects of the target company's business and assets, ensuring that buyers receive assurances about key areas of concern.

Warranties, on the other hand, are assurances about the future performance or condition of the target company's business and assets. Sellers warrant that certain conditions will continue to hold true following the closing of the transaction, providing buyers with protection against unexpected developments or changes that may occur post-closing.

Effective negotiation of representations and warranties requires careful consideration of the risks and uncertainties associated with the transaction, as well as the interests and objectives of both parties. Buyers seek robust representations and warranties to protect against potential liabilities, risks, and losses that may arise from undisclosed issues or inaccuracies in the information provided by the seller. Sellers, on the other hand, aim to limit their exposure and liability by qualifying or narrowing the scope of representations and warranties, and by establishing caps, baskets, and other limitations on indemnification obligations.

Arlind, as an experienced M&A Adviser with an entrepreneur background, brings a unique perspective and expertise to the negotiation of representations and warranties. With his firsthand experience as an entrepreneur, Arlind understands the challenges and complexities of running a business and can anticipate the concerns and priorities of both buyers and sellers. His entrepreneurial background enables him to assess the risks and opportunities associated with the transaction from a practical, real-world perspective, allowing him to provide valuable insights and guidance to his clients.

Arlind's expertise in M&A transactions equips him with the knowledge and skills necessary to navigate the complexities of negotiating representations and warranties effectively. He can help clients identify key areas of concern, craft tailored representations and warranties that address specific risks and uncertainties, and negotiate favorable terms and conditions that protect their interests and achieve their objectives.

Representations and warranties play a crucial role in M&A transactions, providing buyers with assurances about the accuracy and completeness of information disclosed by the seller. Effective negotiation of representations and warranties requires careful consideration of the risks and uncertainties associated with the transaction, as well as the interests and objectives of both parties. With Arlind's expertise and entrepreneurial background, clients can navigate the negotiation process with confidence, knowing that their interests are protected and their objectives are being pursued diligently.

Skeletons in the Closet and Indemnification:

In the intricate world of mergers and acquisitions (M&A), indemnification provisions serve as crucial safeguards to protect both buyers and sellers against unforeseen risks and liabilities that may arise during or after the transaction. These contractual mechanisms allocate responsibility for losses or liabilities stemming from breaches of representations, warranties, or other contractual obligations, providing parties with recourse in the event of unexpected developments or undisclosed issues.

At the heart of indemnification provisions lies the principle of accountability and risk allocation. Sellers typically indemnify buyers against losses resulting from misrepresentations or breaches of warranties made in the purchase agreement. These assurances provide buyers with recourse in case the target company's representations or warranties are found to be inaccurate or incomplete, thereby protecting their investment and mitigating risks.

On the other hand, buyers may also provide indemnification to sellers for certain specified risks or liabilities, such as undisclosed liabilities, pending litigation, or contingent liabilities. By offering indemnification, buyers provide sellers with assurances that they will be protected against unforeseen risks or liabilities that may arise post-closing, thereby incentivizing sellers to disclose any potential issues upfront and facilitating transparency and trust between the parties.

Indemnification provisions are carefully negotiated and drafted to address specific risks and liabilities relevant to the transaction. These provisions typically outline the scope of indemnification, including the types of losses or liabilities covered, the duration of indemnity obligations, any limitations or exclusions to indemnification, and procedures for making indemnification claims and resolving disputes.

Effective negotiation of indemnification provisions requires parties to assess the risks and uncertainties associated with the transaction and allocate responsibility accordingly. Buyers seek robust indemnification provisions to protect against potential losses or liabilities that may arise from undisclosed issues or breaches of representations and warranties, while sellers aim to limit their exposure and preserve their assets by negotiating limitations on indemnification obligations.

Indemnification provisions play a crucial role in shaping the overall risk allocation between buyers and sellers in an M&A transaction. By delineating the responsibilities and obligations of each party, these provisions provide clarity and certainty regarding the allocation of risks and liabilities, thereby minimizing uncertainties and facilitating the smooth execution of the transaction.

Indemnification provisions are essential components of M&A transactions, providing parties with recourse in the event of unexpected developments or undisclosed issues. These provisions serve to allocate responsibility for losses or liabilities arising from breaches of representations, warranties, or other contractual obligations, thereby protecting the interests of both buyers and sellers and facilitating transparency, trust, and certainty in the transaction. Effective negotiation and drafting of indemnification provisions require parties to carefully assess the risks and uncertainties associated with the transaction and allocate responsibility accordingly, ensuring a fair and equitable outcome for all parties involved.

Almost There (I Promise!) - Escrow:
As the final stages of a merger or acquisition (M&A) transaction unfold, parties often find themselves on the cusp of completing the deal, with only a few remaining hurdles to overcome. Among these, one of the most crucial aspects is the establishment of escrow arrangements. Escrow involves the deposit of funds or documents with a neutral third party, known as an escrow agent, pending the satisfaction of certain conditions or obligations. Escrow accounts serve as a safeguard to ensure that funds are available to address post-closing contingencies or disputes, providing security and assurance to both parties involved in the transaction.

At its core, an escrow arrangement acts as a mechanism to mitigate risks and uncertainties associated with the transaction's completion. By depositing funds or documents into escrow, parties create a level of security and assurance that certain obligations will be fulfilled, or certain conditions will be met, before the funds are released or the documents are transferred to the intended recipient. This serves to protect the interests of both the buyer and the seller, providing a neutral ground where assets can be held until all parties are satisfied with the terms of the transaction.

Escrow arrangements are commonly used in M&A transactions to address a variety of scenarios and contingencies. For example, in cases where the seller has made representations and warranties about the target company's financial health or legal compliance, funds may be held in escrow to cover any potential breaches or inaccuracies discovered after the closing. Similarly, escrow may be used to hold back a portion of the purchase price to ensure that certain post-closing obligations, such as indemnification claims or earn-out payments, are fulfilled as agreed upon.

The role of the escrow agent is crucial in ensuring the integrity and effectiveness of the escrow arrangement. The escrow agent acts as a neutral third party entrusted with safeguarding the deposited funds or documents and administering the escrow account in accordance with the terms of the agreement. The escrow agent remains impartial and independent, facilitating communication between the parties and ensuring that the escrow funds are released or the documents are transferred only when all conditions are met.

In addition to providing security and assurance, escrow arrangements also streamline the closing process by reducing the need for parties to hold funds or documents in their own accounts pending the completion of the transaction. This helps expedite the transfer of assets and ensures that the transaction proceeds smoothly and efficiently, without unnecessary delays or complications.

Escrow arrangements play a vital role in the final stages of an M&A transaction, providing security and assurance to both parties involved. By depositing funds or documents with a neutral third party, parties create a mechanism to address post-closing contingencies or disputes, mitigating risks and uncertainties associated with the transaction's completion. With the assistance of an experienced escrow agent, parties can navigate the complexities of escrow arrangements with confidence, ensuring that their interests are protected and the transaction proceeds smoothly and efficiently.

You Made It - Closing Day:
After weeks or even months of negotiations, due diligence, and preparations, closing day finally arrives—the moment when all the hard work and efforts invested in the merger or acquisition (M&A) transaction come to fruition. Closing day represents the culmination of the transaction, where parties come together to execute the final documents, transfer ownership of the target company, and exchange consideration. This pivotal moment marks the official transition of control and responsibility from the seller to the buyer, signaling the beginning of a new chapter for the acquired business.

The closing process typically unfolds through a formal closing meeting attended by representatives from both parties, including legal counsel, financial advisors, and other key stakeholders. During this meeting, parties review and execute the final versions of the purchase agreement, ancillary documents, and any other closing-related paperwork. Signatures are affixed, documents are exchanged, and consideration is transferred, solidifying the legal and financial aspects of the transaction.

Depending on the preferences and arrangements of the parties involved, closing day may take place in person, with all parties gathered in a boardroom or conference room, or through electronic means, with documents exchanged and signatures obtained remotely. Regardless of the format, the overarching goal remains the same—to ensure that all necessary steps are taken to finalize the transaction and effectuate the transfer of ownership in accordance with the terms of the purchase agreement.

Throughout the closing process, Arlind, as an experienced M&A Adviser, will be there every step of the way to provide guidance, support, and assistance to his clients. With his expertise and industry knowledge, Arlind can navigate the complexities of the closing process, anticipate potential issues or challenges, and ensure that all necessary documents are prepared, reviewed, and executed accurately and efficiently.

Arlind's presence during the closing day serves as a reassuring presence for his clients, providing them with peace of mind and confidence that their interests are being protected and their objectives are being pursued diligently. Whether it's facilitating communication between parties, addressing last-minute concerns, or overseeing the execution of closing documents, Arlind's role as an M&A Adviser is instrumental in ensuring that the closing process proceeds smoothly and successfully.

Closing day represents the culmination of the M&A transaction, where parties finalize the details of the deal and transfer ownership of the target company. With Arlind by their side, clients can navigate the complexities of the closing process with confidence, knowing that they have a trusted advisor advocating for their interests and guiding them through every step of the journey.

After the Closing:
The closing of a merger or acquisition (M&A) transaction marks the end of one chapter and the beginning of another—the journey of integrating the acquired business into the buyer's operations and realizing the anticipated synergies and benefits of the transaction. While closing day represents a significant milestone, it is essential to recognize that the work does not end there. Post-closing considerations play a crucial role in ensuring a smooth transition and maximizing the value of the transaction for all parties involved.

One of the primary post-closing considerations is integrating the acquired business into the buyer's operations seamlessly. This may involve aligning organizational structures, streamlining business processes, integrating IT systems and technologies, and harmonizing cultures and values. Effective integration is essential for capturing synergies, minimizing disruptions, and maximizing operational efficiencies, ultimately enhancing the overall value of the combined entity.

Additionally, all parties must fulfill any remaining obligations under the purchase agreement, including post-closing adjustments, earn-out payments, or indemnification claims. This may require ongoing communication and cooperation between the buyer and the seller to address any outstanding issues or disputes promptly and amicably. Clear and open lines of communication are essential for maintaining trust and goodwill between the parties and resolving any post-closing challenges efficiently. Effective post-closing management is essential for preserving and enhancing the value of the acquired business over the long term. This may involve implementing strategic initiatives to drive growth and profitability, optimizing resource allocation, and fostering a culture of innovation and continuous improvement. Arlind, as an experienced M&A Adviser, brings a wealth of expertise in marketing, IT, investments, and business growth to the table. His insights and guidance can help buyers navigate the complexities of post-closing integration and management, identifying opportunities for value creation and strategic expansion. Arlind's expertise and industry knowledge can add value beyond the immediate post-closing phase, maintaining lasting relationships with clients and supporting their growth and expansion initiatives in local, national, or international markets. Whether it's exploring new market opportunities, expanding product lines, or pursuing strategic partnerships, Arlind can provide invaluable advice and support to help clients achieve their business objectives and maximize the value of their investments.

In conclusion, post-closing considerations are essential for ensuring a smooth transition and maximizing the value of an M&A transaction. With Arlind by their side, clients can navigate the complexities of post-closing integration and management with confidence, knowing that they have a trusted advisor advocating for their interests and guiding them every step of the way. Arlind's expertise in marketing, IT, investments, and business growth adds value beyond the transaction, helping clients maintain lasting relationships and achieve their long-term strategic objectives. This highlights the significance of "The Closing" in the merger or acquisition process, where parties finalize the transaction and transfer ownership of the target company. By understanding the closing process, preparing diligently, negotiating effectively, and addressing key considerations such as representations, warranties, indemnification, escrow, and post-closing management, parties can navigate the complexities of M&A transactions with confidence and achieve successful outcomes.

Final Thoughts

Embarking on the journey of mergers and acquisitions (M&A) is akin to navigating a complex and dynamic landscape, filled with challenges, opportunities, and uncertainties. From the initial contemplation of strategic objectives to the final moments of closing the deal, every step in the M&A process requires careful consideration, strategic planning, and effective execution. As we reflect on the journey from beginning to end, several key themes emerge, shaping our understanding of the M&A process and its implications for businesses and stakeholders.

At the outset, the decision to pursue an M&A transaction is driven by a myriad of strategic considerations, including expansion into new markets, diversification of product offerings, consolidation of market share, or realization of synergies. This initial phase involves evaluating strategic objectives, assessing market opportunities, and identifying potential targets or opportunities for growth. It requires foresight, vision, and a clear understanding of the organization's long-term goals and aspirations.

As the journey progresses, the process of identifying, evaluating, and negotiating with potential buyers or sellers becomes paramount. This phase involves conducting thorough due diligence, negotiating terms and conditions, and navigating complex legal and financial considerations. It requires diligence, perseverance, and effective communication to overcome challenges, address concerns, and reach mutually beneficial agreements that create value for all parties involved.

Throughout the M&A process, maintaining confidentiality, managing expectations, and fostering trust and transparency are essential for building strong relationships and navigating negotiations effectively. Whether it's negotiating the purchase agreement, addressing representations and warranties, or finalizing closing documents, the success of the transaction hinges on the ability of parties to collaborate, compromise, and find common ground amidst competing interests and objectives.

As the journey nears its conclusion, the final moments of closing the deal represent a culmination of months, if not years, of hard work, dedication, and perseverance. Closing day symbolizes the realization of strategic objectives, the fulfillment of aspirations, and the beginning of a new chapter for the parties involved. It is a moment of celebration, reflection, and anticipation for the future, as parties come together to execute final documents, transfer ownership, and exchange consideration.

However, the journey does not end with the closing of the deal; rather, it marks the beginning of a new phase of integration, growth, and value creation. Post-closing management, integration planning, and ongoing communication are essential for ensuring a smooth transition and maximizing the value of the transaction over the long term. It requires adaptability, resilience, and a commitment to continuous improvement to navigate the challenges and capitalize on the opportunities that arise.

The journey of mergers and acquisitions is a transformative experience that shapes the trajectory of organizations, industries, and economies. From the initial contemplation of strategic objectives to the final moments of closing the deal and beyond, every step in the process requires vision, leadership, and collaboration to achieve success. As we reflect on the journey from beginning to end, we recognize the importance of strategic planning, effective execution, and unwavering commitment to realizing our goals and aspirations in the dynamic and competitive landscape of M&A.

Arlind Sadiku, an experienced M&A Advisor & Broker, he stands as a guiding force in the intricate world of mergers and acquisitions (M&A), offering indispensable expertise and strategic acumen to both buyers and sellers alike. His vast knowledge, honed over years of navigating diverse industries, coupled with his multilingual capabilities, positions him as a trusted partner capable of facilitating successful transactions across various regions, including the USA, EU, UK, and UAE.

Arlind's journey in the realm of entrepreneurship spans over a quarter-century, during which he has co-founded multiple businesses across diverse sectors such as commercial real estate, hospitality, marketing, and artificial intelligence (AI). This wealth of entrepreneurial experience grants him a deep understanding of the intricacies of business operations, financial dynamics, and market nuances, enabling him to provide invaluable insights and guidance to his clients.

In the realm of M&A, Arlind's role is multifaceted and crucial. For sellers, he offers tailored strategies to maximize the value of their businesses, drawing upon his expertise to conduct thorough valuation analyses, develop targeted marketing plans, and navigate negotiations with potential buyers. His extensive network of industry contacts allows him to effectively position businesses in the marketplace, ensuring optimal exposure and attracting qualified buyers.

For buyers seeking strategic acquisitions, Arlind serves as a trusted advisor, assisting them in identifying suitable targets that align with their objectives and investment criteria. His deep understanding of various industries enables him to conduct comprehensive due diligence assessments, evaluate potential risks and opportunities, and structure deals in a manner that maximizes value and minimizes risks.

One of Arlind's unique strengths lies in his expertise in franchising, boasting a network of over 500 franchises. This specialization allows him to offer tailored guidance to both franchisors and franchisees, facilitating successful transactions and fostering growth within the franchising ecosystem. Arlind's multilingual proficiency further enhances his ability to navigate the complexities of global M&A transactions, facilitating seamless communication and collaboration with clients and stakeholders from diverse cultural backgrounds. Whether it's negotiating deal terms, coordinating due diligence efforts, or navigating regulatory requirements, Adam's linguistic skills enable him to bridge cultural and linguistic barriers, fostering trust and facilitating successful outcomes.

Arlind's role as an M&A Advisor & Broker extends far beyond mere transaction facilitation. He serves as a strategic partner, leveraging his extensive experience, industry knowledge, and multilingual capabilities to empower clients to achieve their M&A objectives, navigate complexities, and unlock value in an ever-evolving global business landscape. With Arlind at their side, buyers and sellers alike can navigate the intricacies of M&A transactions with confidence, knowing they have a seasoned expert guiding them every step of the way. Arlind is an author who has published several books that are available for purchase on Amazon and Google.

For Sellers:

Strategic Planning: Arlind assists sellers in developing a comprehensive M&A strategy tailored to their specific objectives and circumstances. He helps sellers evaluate their options, identify potential buyers, and determine the optimal timing for the sale of their business.

Valuation Analysis: Arlind conducts thorough valuation analyses to determine the fair market value of the seller's business. By considering various factors such as financial performance, market trends, and industry benchmarks, he provides sellers with a realistic assessment of their business's worth.

Marketing and Positioning: Arlind creates customized marketing strategies to promote the seller's business to potential buyers. He leverages his extensive network and industry connections to identify qualified buyers and effectively position the business in the marketplace.

Negotiation Support: Arlind serves as a skilled negotiator on behalf of the seller, advocating for their best interests throughout the negotiation process. He helps sellers navigate complex deal terms, address buyer concerns, and secure favorable terms and conditions for the sale.

Due Diligence Management: Arlind coordinates the due diligence process, ensuring that all necessary information and documentation are provided to potential buyers in a timely and organized manner. He helps sellers address any concerns or inquiries raised during due diligence, minimizing delays and maximizing deal certainty.

For Buyers:

Target Identification: Arlind assists buyers in identifying suitable acquisition targets that align with their strategic objectives and investment criteria. He conducts thorough market research and target screening to identify opportunities that offer growth potential and value creation.

Deal Structuring: Arlind advises buyers on deal structuring and financing options to optimize the terms of the transaction. He helps buyers evaluate different acquisition structures, assess financing alternatives, and develop creative solutions to overcome potential obstacles.

Due Diligence Support: Arlind guides buyers through the due diligence process, helping them assess the risks and opportunities associated with the target company. He conducts comprehensive due diligence reviews, identifies key issues, and provides strategic insights to inform the decision-making process.

Negotiation Assistance: Arlind represents buyers in negotiations with sellers, leveraging his negotiation expertise to secure favorable terms and pricing for the acquisition. He advocates for the buyer's interests while maintaining a collaborative approach to facilitate successful deal outcomes.

Post-Acquisition Integration: Arlind provides post-acquisition integration support to ensure a smooth transition and maximize the value of the acquisition. He helps buyers develop integration plans, align organizational cultures, and implement synergies to drive operational efficiency and growth.

Overall, Adam's role as an M&A advisor is to guide both buyers and sellers through every stage of the M&A process, from initial planning and due diligence to negotiation and post-deal integration. His expertise, professionalism, and dedication to client success make him a trusted partner for navigating the complexities of M&A transactions.

Arlind Sadiku

www.arlindsadiku.com

M&A Acronyms and Language

AM: Acquisition Memorandum
BOD: Board of Directors
CIM: Confidential Information Memorandum
DCF: Discounted Cash Flow
EBITDA: Earnings Before Interest, Taxes, Depreciation, and Amortization
FCF: Free Cash Flow
GAAP: Generally Accepted Accounting Principles
HR: Human Resources
IPO: Initial Public Offering
JV: Joint Venture
KPI: Key Performance Indicator
LOI: Letter of Intent
M&A: Mergers and Acquisitions
NDAs: Non-Disclosure Agreements
OPM: Other People's Money
P&L: Profit and Loss
QoQ: Quarter over Quarter
ROFR: Right of First Refusal
SPA: Share Purchase Agreement
TTM: Trailing Twelve Months
UCC: Uniform Commercial Code
VDR: Virtual Data Room
WACC: Weighted Average Cost of Capital
XM: Exit Multiples
YTD: Year to Date
Z-Score: Altman Z-Score
ERP: Enterprise Resource Planning
CFO: Chief Financial Officer
CTA: Call to Action
EOM: End of Month
LBO: Leveraged Buyout
MOU: Memorandum of Understanding
EOM: End of Month
CAGR: Compound Annual Growth Rate
MBO: Management Buyout

RFP: Request for Proposal
HSR: Hart-Scott-Rodino Act
MAC: Material Adverse Change
ESOP: Employee Stock Ownership Plan
PEG: Private Equity Group
EPC: Earnout Payment Calculation
CVR: Contingent Value Rights
CMS: Content Management System
PPC: Pay Per Click
VC: Venture Capital
ROI: Return on Investment
SaaS: Software as a Service
TAM: Total Addressable Market
EoY: End of Year
DD: Due Diligence
SPA: Sale and Purchase Agreement
B2B: Business to Business
B2C: Business to Consumer
CRM: Customer Relationship Management
PEG: Private Equity Group
API: Application Programming Interface
CTA: Call to Action
KPO: Knowledge Process Outsourcing
LOA: Letter of Agreement
NAICS: North American Industry Classification System
OTC: Over the Counter
PEG: Private Equity Group
Q&A: Question and Answer
RTO: Reverse Takeover
SOW: Statement of Work
TTM: Trailing Twelve Months
VPA: Virtual Private Agreement
WSO: Wall Street Oasis
YTM: Yield to Maturity
ZBB: Zero-Based Budgeting
ABL: Asset-Based Lending
BDC: Business Development Company
CDO: Collateralized Debt Obligation

EBIT: Earnings Before Interest and Taxes
FOB: Free on Board
G&A: General and Administrative
HHI: Herfindahl-Hirschman Index
IRR: Internal Rate of Return
JVs: Joint Ventures
KYC: Know Your Customer
LTM: Last Twelve Months
MTM: Mark to Market
NOL: Net Operating Loss
OID: Original Issue Discount
PEG: Private Equity Group
R&D: Research and Development
SOW: Statement of Work
T&E: Travel and Entertainment
VIE: Variable Interest Entity
WIP: Work in Progress
ZTA: Zero Tolerance Approach
AAR: Asset Acquisition Report
BBP: Business Blueprint
CTA: Call to Action
DIP: Debtor-In-Possession
EOM: End of Month
FDD: Franchise Disclosure Document
GFC: Global Financial Crisis
HMA: Hostile M&A
IRR: Internal Rate of Return
JV: Joint Venture
KPI: Key Performance Indicator
LOI: Letter of Intent
M&A: Mergers and Acquisitions
NDA: Non-Disclosure Agreement
OPM: Other People's Money
P/E: Price to Earnings
QoQ: Quarter over Quarter
ROA: Return on Assets
SaaS: Software as a Service
TTM: Trailing Twelve Months

UCC: Uniform Commercial Code
VDR: Virtual Data Room
WACC: Weighted Average Cost of Capital
XIRR: Extended Internal Rate of Return
YTM: Yield to Maturity
AUM: Assets Under Management
B2B: Business to Business
CAGR: Compound Annual Growth Rate
DDM: Dividend Discount Model
EPL: Employee Provident Fund
FDI: Foreign Direct Investment
GNP: Gross National Product
HFT: High-Frequency Trading
IRR: Internal Rate of Return
JDA: Joint Development Agreement
KFS: Key Financials
LCA: Letter of Credit Agreement
MNC: Multinational Corporation
NPA: Non-Performing Asset
OBO: Offer by Owner
P/E: Price to Earnings Ratio
QIP: Qualified Institutional Placement
ROE: Return on Equity
SAR: Stock Appreciation Rights
TQM: Total Quality Management
UPI: Unified Payments Interface
VEP: Variable Earnings Per Share
WIP: Work In Progress
XIRR: Extended Internal Rate of Return
YTM: Yield to Maturity
ZIRP: Zero Interest Rate Policy
AM: Asset Management
BPO: Business Process Outsourcing
CCI: Competition Commission of India
DSS: Decision Support System
EFC: Equity Financing Costs
FTE: Full-Time Equivalent
GDP: Gross Domestic Product

HPA: High-Potential Acquisition
IPO: Initial Public Offering
JPA: Joint Partnership Agreement
KSA: Key Success Areas
LBO: Leveraged Buyout
NDA: Non-Disclosure Agreement
OTC: Over the Counter
P&L: Profit and Loss
QRM: Qualitative Risk Management
ROI: Return on Investment
SAR: Specific Absorption Rate
TCO: Total Cost of Ownership
UPI: Unified Payments Interface
VBM: Value-Based Management
WACC: Weighted Average Cost of Capital
XIRR: Extended Internal Rate of Return
YTM: Yield to Maturity
ABA: American Bankers Association
BCG: Boston Consulting Group
CDO: Collateralized Debt Obligation
DIP: Debtor in Possession
EIR: Effective Interest Rate
FDI: Foreign Direct Investment
GNP: Gross National Product
HHI: Herfindahl-Hirschman Index
IRR: Internal Rate of Return
JVs: Joint Ventures
KPO: Knowledge Process Outsourcing
LBO: Leveraged Buyout
M&A: Mergers and Acquisitions
NDA: Non-Disclosure Agreement
OPM: Other People's Money
P&L: Profit and Loss
QoQ: Quarter over Quarter
ROA: Return on Assets
TTM: Trailing Twelve Months
UCC: Uniform Commercial Code
VDR: Virtual Data Room

WACC: Weighted Average Cost of Capital
XIRR: Extended Internal Rate of Return
YTM: Yield to Maturity
Z-Score: Altman Z-Score
ABL: Asset-Based Lending
BDC: Business Development Company
CDO: Collateralized Debt Obligation
EBIT: Earnings Before Interest and Taxes
FOB: Free on Board
G&A: General and Administrative
HHI: Herfindahl-Hirschman Index
IRR: Internal Rate of Return
JVs: Joint Ventures
KYC: Know Your Customer
LTM: Last Twelve Months
MTM: Mark to Market
NOL: Net Operating Loss
OID: Original Issue Discount
PEG: Private Equity Group
R&D: Research and Development
SOW: Statement of Work
T&E: Travel and Entertainment
VIE: Variable Interest Entity
WIP: Work in Progress
ZTA: Zero Tolerance Approach
AAR: Asset Acquisition Report
BBP: Business Blueprint
CTA: Call to Action
DIP: Debtor-In-Possession
EOM: End of Month
FDD: Franchise Disclosure Document
GFC: Global Financial Crisis
HMA: Hostile M&A
IRR: Internal Rate of Return
KPI: Key Performance Indicator
LOI: Letter of Intent
M&A: Mergers and Acquisitions
NDA: Non-Disclosure Agreement

OPM: Other People's Money
P/E: Price to Earnings
QoQ: Quarter over Quarter
ROA: Return on Assets
TTM: Trailing Twelve Months
UCC: Uniform Commercial Code
VDR: Virtual Data Room
WACC: Weighted Average Cost of Capital
XIRR: Extended Internal Rate of Return
YTM: Yield to Maturity
AUM: Assets Under Management
B2B: Business to Business
CAGR: Compound Annual Growth Rate
DDM: Dividend Discount Model
EPL: Employee Provident Fund
FDI: Foreign Direct Investment
GNP: Gross National Product
HFT: High-Frequency Trading
IRR: Internal Rate of Return
JDA: Joint Development Agreement
KFS: Key Financials
LCA: Letter of Credit Agreement
MNC: Multinational Corporation
NPA: Non-Performing Asset
OBO: Offer by Owner
P/E: Price to Earnings Ratio
QIP: Qualified Institutional Placement
ROE: Return on Equity
SAR: Stock Appreciation Rights
TQM: Total Quality Management
UPI: Unified Payments Interface
VEP: Variable Earnings Per Share
WIP: Work In Progress
XIRR: Extended Internal Rate of Return
YTM: Yield to Maturity
ZIRP: Zero Interest Rate Policy
AM: Asset Management
BPO: Business Process Outsourcing

CCI: Competition Commission of India
DSS: Decision Support System
EFC: Equity Financing Costs
FTE: Full-Time Equivalent
GDP: Gross Domestic Product
HPA: High-Potential Acquisition
IPO: Initial Public Offering
JPA: Joint Partnership Agreement
KSA: Key Success Areas
LBO: Leveraged Buyout
M&A: Mergers and Acquisitions
NDA: Non-Disclosure Agreement
OTC: Over the Counter
P&L: Profit and Loss
QRM: Qualitative Risk Management
ROI: Return on Investment
SAR: Specific Absorption Rate
TCO: Total Cost of Ownership
UPI: Unified Payments Interface
VBM: Value-Based Management
WACC: Weighted Average Cost of Capital
XIRR: Extended Internal Rate of Return
YTM: Yield to Maturity
Z-Score: Altman Z-Score
ABA: American Bankers Association
BCG: Boston Consulting Group
CDO: Collateralized Debt Obligation
DIP: Debtor in Possession
EIR: Effective Interest Rate
FDI: Foreign Direct Investment
GNP: Gross National Product
HHI: Herfindahl-Hirschman Index
IRR: Internal Rate of Return
JVs: Joint Ventures
KPO: Knowledge Process Outsourcing
LBO: Leveraged Buyout
M&A: Mergers and Acquisitions
NDA: Non-Disclosure Agreement

OPM: Other People's Money
P&L: Profit and Loss
QoQ: Quarter over Quarter
ROA: Return on Assets
SaaS: Software as a Service
TTM: Trailing Twelve Months
UCC: Uniform Commercial Code
WACC: Weighted Average Cost of Capital
XIRR: Extended Internal Rate of Return
YTM: Yield to Maturity
ABL: Asset-Based Lending
BDC: Business Development Company
CDO: Collateralized Debt Obligation
FOB: Free on Board
G&A: General and Administrative
HHI: Herfindahl-Hirschman Index
IRR: Internal Rate of Return
JVs: Joint Ventures
KYC: Know Your Customer
LTM: Last Twelve Months
MTM: Mark to Market
NOL: Net Operating Loss
SDE: Seller's Discretionary .

www.ingramcontent.com/pod-product-compliance
Lightning Source LLC
Chambersburg PA
CBHW070153230526
45471CB00002B/645